# A Midsummer Knight

*Reflections On Life and Living*
by
**Jim McGuiggan**

*To Stan Cunningham*
*who loves the Lord Jesus Christ*
*and our daughter Linda*

© *Copyright 2011 Jim McGuiggan. All rights reserved.*

*No part of this book may be reproduced, stored in a retrieval system, or transmitted by any means without the written permission of the author.*

*Printed in the United States of America.*

*This book is printed on acid-free paper.*

## Table of Contents

Chapter 1 MIDSUMMER KNIGHT ..................................................... 5
Chapter 2 HOW'D YOU DO THAT? ................................................. 7
Chapter 3 AS GOOD AS IT GETS ..................................................... 11
Chapter 4 WHAT DAY WAS THAT? ................................................. 13
Chapter 5 DANCING WITHOUT MUSIC ......................................... 15
Chapter 6 I KNOW SOMEONE ........................................................ 19
Chapter 7 NOT ON THEIR WATCH ................................................ 21
Chapter 8 A LETTER TO A VERY ILL FRIEND ............................... 23
Chapter 9 LIFE IN STRANGE PLACES ............................................ 25
Chapter 10 AWAY FROM HOME ..................................................... 27
Chapter 11 WHICH GOD EXISTS? .................................................. 29
Chapter 12 HAMMERS AND SCALPELS ........................................ 31
Chapter 13 LEAVE NO DOUBT ....................................................... 35
Chapter 14 THE WIND OF THE SPIRIT ......................................... 39
Chapter 15 THE TYRANT'S SULK ................................................... 43
Chapter 16 MEANINGLESS! MEANINGLESS! ............................... 47
Chapter 17 PUDDLEGLUM .............................................................. 51
Chapter 18 THE GOSPEL AND THE UNLUCKY ........................... 53
Chapter 19 DIALOGUE WITH DEATH .......................................... 59
Chapter 20 GOOD AND FAITHFUL SERVANT ............................. 63
Chapter 21 DR. JEKYLL & MR. HYDE ............................................ 65
Chapter 22 JESUS CHRIST AND CAMELOT ................................. 67
Chapter 23 A JOYFUL AND ADEQUATE JESUS ........................... 71
Chapter 24 THERE'S NO GOD—SO WHAT? ................................. 73
Chapter 25 THE DEATH OF A CHILD ........................................... 77
Chapter 26 PERSONAL FAITH AND CHRIST'S TRIUMPH ........ 81
Chapter 27 BURNING BUSHES & GOING BAREFOOT .............. 85
Chapter 28 NATURAL CALAMITIES & ETERNAL TORMENT ... 87

Chapter 29 THIS I BELIEVE ............................................................................. 89
Chapter 30 THE TREES WILL CLAP THEIR HANDS .................................. 93
Chapter 31 WILL THE CREATION ABIDE FOREVER? ............................... 97
Chapter 32 THE CREATION IS "FOR" JESUS............................................ 103
Chapter33 WHAT'S CHRISTIAN ABOUT CHRISTIAN FAITH?............ 105
Chapter 34 SETTLING FOR LESS ............................................................... 109
Chapter 35 ANGELS WITH DIRTY FACES ................................................ 111
Chapter 36 A WAR FOR HEROES ............................................................... 115
Chapter 37 GEORGE DAWSON'S MULE AND WAGON ........................ 119
Chapter 38 "DUZ YIR MAJESTY KNOW..." .............................................. 121
Chapter 39 I FELT LIKE DANCING ............................................................ 125
Chapter 40 ABEL MAGWITCH .................................................................. 127
Chapter 41 CRIPPLED TRUTHS WILL WALK .......................................... 131
Chapter 42 A VOICE IN FAR-FLUNG GALAXIES.................................... 133
Chapter 43 PARADISE CAN BE HERE TOO.............................................. 135
Chapter 44 IT MATTERS TO GOD!............................................................. 139
Chapter 45 WHAT WE HAVE TO OFFER .................................................. 141

# 1

## A MIDSUMMER KNIGHT

O'Henry tells of Gaines, "the man who said he thought New York was the finest summer resort in the country." While others moaned and melted in the heat, dived for the shade or an electric fan, and wished for the mountains, he mocked the notion of going to the woods to eat canned goods from the city, being wakened in the morning by a million flies, getting soaked to the skin catching the tiniest fish and struggling up perpendicular cliffs. No sir, he preferred to stay at home. If he wanted fish, he'd go to a cool restaurant—home comforts, that's what he chose, while the fools spent half their summer driving to and from their spartan locations with all the modern inconveniences.

A friend urged him to come with him for two weeks to Beaverkill, where the fish were jumping at anything that even looked like a fly. He said a mutual friend, Harding, had caught a three-pound brown trout—but Gaines was having none of it. "Nonsense!" he's snort and then off to his office to plunge himself into a mountain of work until late in the afternoon when, with feet up on his desk, he mused to himself: "I wonder what kind of bait Harding used."

The man who said he thought that New York was the finest summer resort in the country dozed off in the stifling heat, was awakened by his mail-bringing clerk, and decided to take a quick look before he left for the day. A few lines of one of them said:

*My Dear Dear Husband:*

*Just received your letter ordering us to stay another month...Rita's cough is almost gone...Johnny has gone wild like a little Indian...it will be the making of both children...work so hard, and I know that your business can hardly afford to keep us here so long...best man that ever...you always pretend that you like the city in summer...trout fishing that you used to be so fond of...and all to keep us well and happy...come to you if it were not doing the babies so much good...I stood last evening on Chimney Rock in exactly the same spot...when you put the wreath of roses on my head...said you would be my true knight...have always been that to me...ever and ever.*

The man, who said he thought New York was the finest summer resort in the country, on his way home in the sweltering summer heat, dropped into a cafe and had a glass of warm beer under an electric fan. "Wonder what kind of a fly old Harding used," he murmured to himself.

I love it when those in love sometimes "tell lies" gallantly. They say things no one believes—least of all themselves. They're forever making sacrifices—some large, some little—to make life easier, finer, lovelier, for those they love...They're in love and they do what lovers have done in every age down the centuries—they give themselves in whatever ways their love and situation calls for. And they do it without trumpets blowing or affected sweetness and they don't wear pained expressions. They'd almost convince you that they really did believe that New York City was the finest summer resort in the country.

[Quoted from my little book called Let Me Count The Ways with permission from Howard Publishing Company, West Monroe, Louisiana, 2001]

# 2

## HOW'D YOU DO THAT?

Jesus was brought up in Nazareth and he moved to Capernaum ("the village of Nahum") and it became a centre of his ministry. There he became noted as a teacher and a healer (Luke 4:16, 23) and it was there that he was stunned by a pagan. Twice in the New Testament we're told that Jesus was astonished and in both cases it had to do with faith.

Luke 7:1-10 tells us of a foreigner, a Roman officer, who despite being a part of the forces of occupation loved Israel and honoured them and as a consequence he was esteemed by the Jewish leaders.

He had a servant he really cared for and that servant was very ill so the foreigner sent Jewish people to ask a favor of this young Jewish prophet. He wanted him to heal the sick man and Jesus was on his way to do just that. Before Christ got to the house the soldier sent word that he didn't mean for Jesus to come to his house, only that he speak and the healing would be done. The soldier said he knew what authority was. He had soldiers under him and he was under others. When he or his superiors spoke the response was immediate—the order was carried out. He saw it as sufficient that

Jesus simply command the disease to leave and it would. Luke 7:9 tells us that Jesus was stunned with amazement and turned to the crowd saying he hadn't seen faith like that in his own nation.

We've become accustomed to the idea that Jesus wept, became angry or was tender, that he was moved with compassion and pity but is there not something astonishing about Jesus being astonished? How did he look when he heard what the centurion had to say? What registered on his face? More important, what are the implications in the fact that he was astonished at the man's great faith?

It suggests that something utterly unexpected had happened, doesn't it? But what are the implications in that? Did Jesus not see himself or his Father as worthy of such trust? No, that wasn't the problem, he knew better than that. What astonished him then? We can guess about the man's pagan raising and that he was living in a town that Jesus cursed for its arrogance and hard heart (Matthew 11:23-24). Maybe that enters in it. Be that as it may, whatever the man's past or present environment, it's clear that Jesus thought it astonishing that such faith could be found in such a person. And that should remind us that it isn't always easy to believe or to believe with deep conviction. If believing and believing profoundly were as simple as hearing the gospel there would be no reason to be astonished. Exodus 6:7 reminds us of that.

That's what's so fine about Jesus Christ. That's what leads millions to not only love him but to like him. He just blurts out his pleasure when he meets up with something glorious and weeps his heart out when he meets something tragic. There's an openness about him that while it makes him vulnerable to his enemies it also makes him adorable to those with eyes to trust him.

Neither Matthew nor Luke gives us a psychological study of Christ on this occasion but it's not hard to see and sense his joy. "Can you beat that?" we can hear him say to the following crowd. He understood very well that faith is God's work in us but it isn't coercive work; the believer is not turned into a mindless robot, he or she must personally and freely give him or herself in the process. And people can choose not to believe (see Mark 6:6). When we come across a believer we come across someone who has gladly allowed God to have his way with them.

All of that's plain enough but still, Jesus was astonished! Given the norm this man shouldn't have that faith. Imagine Jesus with his eyes shining, turning to the centurion (compare Matthew 8:13), smiling and saying, "How'd you do that?" We can easily imagine Christ looking intently at him, the pleased surprise still there as he took in the character of the man in front of him. Nor is it hard to imagine the centurion saying, "Oh, sir, we both know that God accomplishes all such things in us." Christ would totally agree but he was still able to thrill at a lovely human response.

We've met people who were raised and continue to live in horrendous circumstances and there they are, up to their hearts in trust. And I don't find it difficult in the least to imagine Christ with joyful astonishment on his face, searching their face for clues, looking at them and asking, "How'd you do that?" And then turning to us, lifted in his spirits by what he has seen, and asking us, "How'd she do that?"

*What Tolkein, Stephen Donaldson and others and can do in fiction, Jesus Christ can do with actual life and truth; things so exciting that we begin to wonder what is truth and what is fiction. He says he came to give us life to the full (John 10:10) and he never lies.*

# 3

## AS GOOD AS IT GETS

I think I know people whose lives are one serious wrestle day after day after day. They get tired! They're physically, emotionally and otherwise worn down and nearly worn out. It isn't something that a good eight-hour sleep will cure (though, God knows, if they could get one of those they'd think it was halfway to Paradise). They've tried all the little social and mental tricks to ease the brain. They're read with deep irritation silly books that tell them every problem in life is part of "the small stuff" that they aren't to sweat and they fling them against the wall in justified impatience. Nonsense books like that are written for people whose lives need nothing more than fine-tuning to make them heavenly. For the really troubled they're a sharp stick in the eye.

In the movie As Good As It Gets Mr. Udhall is a man with serious problems (pleasantly made to look funny in the movie) of the compulsive behavioural kind. Beneath his rudeness, self-centredness and sheerly insulting behaviour is someone who wishes he was free and at peace like so many others around him. Because of his inner turmoil he resents the harmony in their lives and so, when he can, he makes them pay dearly for their good fortune. This further isolates him and screws the coffin lid down a bit tighter on him.

But he's demented and sometimes his excessive ordering of his ways doesn't help and his pain makes him scream out for help. He bursts into the doctor's office and is promptly told to leave without consultation and as he leaves through the crowded waiting room he looks at the people lining the walls. Their unmet needs are written all over their faces and in their body language as they lounge dispiritedly. He says to them, "What if this is as good as it gets?"

Whatever the shortcomings of the movie it is truly worth watching. It's a movie about redemption—the three main characters are redeemed and given a new lease on life. Yes, all right, it's what sick Hollywood normally does—it speaks of redemption without God, without change of character and a redemption that is accomplished by humans all by themselves. I see that and dislike it, and protest it, but I'm not going to apologise for being pleased at seeing things take a fine turn for unhappy people.

And for Udhall things take a lovely turn. I have no wise pieces of advice for people who live with the screws tightening on their hearts that'll make them think that liver cancer is a fine thing or that the fragmentation in their family is small stuff they shouldn't sweat. But I have heard what millions of others have hear, I have heard Someone say that if we give our lives to him, that life as it now is and life without him is not as good as it gets! He can take even our pain and sense of loss and make it into some more than hurt, something more than loss. He can show us that it is more than it seems. What Tolkein, Stephen Donaldson and others and can do in fiction, Jesus Christ can do with actual life and truth; things so exciting that we begin to wonder what is truth and what is fiction. He says he came to give us life to the full (John 10:10) and he never lies. Listen, he offers forgiveness, full and free, but it's fullness of life that he offers and forgiveness is only one aspect of that.

# 4

## WHAT DAY WAS THAT?

*"Today you will be with me in Paradise!"*
*Who said that?*
*"Before this day is out, you'll be with me in Paradise."*
*Who said that? What day was that?*

The massive crowds were singing his praises, the church leaders urged their flocks to come with them to hear him, his friends glowed in admiration and pride for their hero, the people with the power supported his cause, good women laughed out loud at the spectacle of it all and the power to heal flowed from him like Niagara! No wonder he thought it was a heavenly day—the world was glorious, his message had been understood and the nations rejoiced in it. No wonder he could speak words of assurance to a desperate man! The world was at his feet.

But was it a day like that? Is that the kind of day it was when he spoke hope and assurance to that desperate and dying man?

Hardly!

*"Today...Paradise!"*

Today! While the legionnaires of the Empire ruled the country and the world, dealing out misery and death as the way to peace and prosperity—that day he said "this very day!"

Today! While lunatic leaders who didn't know what they were doing yet knew how wise it was to railroad an innocent man to death to maintain the status quo.

Today! While he hung on a public gallows, thirsty, streaked with spit and sweat and blood, rejected by his own people, dismissed as another failed rebel by Rome, deserted by his closest friends and abandoned by his Holy Father?

Arrrgh! What nonsense he spoke!

He spoke as if he was in control. But how could he be in control, for pity's sake, when there he hangs on a public gallows, with a raging thirst and helpless women sobbing their hearts out?

Yes, it's awfully sweet. The way he spoke tenderly to that poor wretch. How it warms the heart. It has that soft chamber-music sound, like something Mendelssohn wrote. It's like something you'd expect in a quiet bedroom; a sad dying one hears a word of warm assurance. "Today you will be with me in Paradise."

But it wasn't a whispered promise in a quiet bedroom, was it? It might even have been half-shouted so that it could be heard above the surge of voices and weeping and hoarse yelling and jeering.

He looked at the rage and the stupidity, the hunger for power and the vested interests and knew exactly what he was looking at and still he claimed that the future lay with him!

If we can't rejoice with that dying thief we're lacking something we desperately need to be fully human, but we need to go beyond what these words of Jesus meant for that poor soul. We need to remember the day on which he spoke such words and what they mean for the world.

He looked at a world that will crucify people—good and bad—and insisted that the future lay in his control. He was making a claim and not just a promise!

Don't let the world fool you! Look at it and acknowledge it as brutal and rapacious and treacherous as it is and can be. And then, if you listen really hard you'll hear:

*"Today...Paradise."*

# 5

## DANCING WITHOUT MUSIC

*"Now the tax collectors and sinners were gathered around to hear him. But the Pharisees and the teachers of the law muttered, 'This man welcomes sinners and eats with them'."* (Luke 15:1-2)

The famous Swiss psychologist, Paul Tournier, confounded those who came from all over the world to learn from him the secret of his phenomenal practice. He insisted he had no special secret and he also insisted that no school of thought had a corner on success. He claimed that it made little or no difference whether the practitioner was a Freudian or followed Maslow, Fromm or the Rogerian non-directional school. He swore that caring for people is what made the difference. The psychological theory was useful up to a point but in the end, Tournier persisted, if the hurting one thought they were being heard and that the person involved with them felt them worthwhile the world was on its way to being changed. It all sounded so commonsensical that the seekers waited for something more specialized and esoteric from him but it never came. To be loved, to be thought worthwhile, and truly enjoyed, is better than all the drugs and the clinical assessments. To believe that someone truly likes to have you around is medicine for every part of us.

So many of us have experienced that. There were things about us that we so detested that we would have spiralled down into emotional oblivion if it hadn't been for certain individuals who loved us. They saw us for what we were and loved us as we were and came to rescue us from painful isolation and self-hatred. They gave us the strength to go on.

But it was no easy job for them. However cranky or rude or even abusive we've been or are we still insist that we have our rights. We might not use the word but we certainly act on it. Everyone owes us and we expect them to come up to it or we'll give them a piece of our mind, even if it's only inside our own head.

If we saw it all happen in a movie on the screen we would think we would recognize immediately that our behaviour was abominable. We would wonder at the patience of those who have stood by us bearing the pain of the abuse and ingratitude day after day after day?

And if we're mistreated, or even think we are, how well we remember the details. We're able to recall the very tone in which the words were spoken (so we think), where we were sitting when it happened and what was said just after that. Instant and complete recall! We who can't remember where we left our keys five minutes ago can recall a six-months-ago complex scene in all its details.

Luke 14:1 tells us this remarkable thing. "One Sabbath, when Jesus went to eat in the house of a prominent Pharisee…" In light of how the religious leaders treated him you might think Jesus would have said, "Thank you but no thanks" when the invitation for dinner came. But no, he graciously accepted even though he knew (as the text goes on to tell us, that he would be "carefully watched"). But we mustn't assume this was "easy" for him to do. That is, Jesus was no machine, programmed by God to run without feelings. Like the rest of us, the temptation to dismiss people was real but he decisively set it aside and did what he thought would please his Father and what was good to others. It's appears that he never treated anyone in such a way that they got the impression that if they were obliterated from off the face of the earth it wouldn't cost him a moment's thought.

And maybe it's this that devastates us most: when someone treats us as though our presence or absence doesn't matter, as though our life or death makes no difference at all to them. And God help us, even if we know we've behaved in such a way as to deserve isolation we're thunderstruck if that's what we get. We keep mistreating people, though we know if someone treated us this way we'd surely walk off; and yet when we're sidelined we're devastated.

Israel complained in Isaiah 64 that God had hidden himself from them. He hadn't done remarkable things for them, and that he was nowhere in sight when they looked for him. In chapter 65 God finds that astonishing and says, "All day long I've held out my hands to a disobedient and argumentative people. I'm even found by people who weren't looking for me." The fault didn't lie in God and maybe most of the time, I'd suppose, the fault doesn't lie in others.

But in fairness, we sort of expect prolonged patience in God. He's up to it. It isn't right but it's the case that we expect him to continue to work with us even though we're consistently a mess. In some ways that makes good sense because if God were the kind of God who would gladly leave us sinking in the muck we would think we've got the wrong God. What makes no sense is for us to keep mistreating other struggling people while expecting them to be God!

But if the story is ever fully told maybe we'll be amazed at how patient and loving some ordinary people have been. These are stories of such grace.

The two lead characters in the movie Awakenings are Leonard Lowe (played by DeNiro) and Doctor Sayers (played by Robin Williams). Lowe as a boy becomes a victim of post-encephalitic syndrome and is cut off from life for about forty years (though he's always conscious that life is going on outside of him). The doctor discovers a drug that brings Leonard out of the dead-zone and he finds life again. The now adult Lowe is astonished at the potential of life and loves it even more now having found it again than he would have if he had never lost it. While exulting in life, within the walls of the hospital Lowe meets a beautiful girl whose father is ill, and the couple are drawn to each other.

Sinister side effects of the drug begin to show. At first twitches and then jerking movements and as it progresses facial distortion and bodily behaviour reminiscent of Huntingdon's chorea. He realises he's sinking and his panic and desperation are only matched by his disgust when he looks at himself. To make matters worse was her gentleness, poise and beauty that only underscored his worsening condition. Though he is now head over heels in love with her he can no longer bear to be in her presence so he plans to sever the tie. Their final meeting in the cafeteria is awkward and during it he insists that he's grotesque though she fervently denies it. Her grace only makes it more difficult for him but he finally says a poignant goodbye (made even more poignant because he shakes her hand in a formal way) as he tells her he doesn't want to see her any more. The truth is he doesn't want her to see him any more. Love for her and self-disgust mingle in that mysterious way they often do in life and it's precisely that mix that drives him against his will to walk away.

He moves from the table jerking violently, face contorted and with chaos in his soul. She follows him, turns him round, takes his hand and slowly but gently and deliberately puts it on her waist and holds the other in her own and begins to dance with him. There's no music, and they're oblivious to the people sitting around, there's just the two of them, he reluctantly and pathetically shuffling and she moulding her steps to his. And that's when the magic wove its spell. Her nearness and grace gradually brought order into his chaotic inner world and what drugs couldn't do she did—the jerking and contortion took their leave and he found peace there in the arms of someone who loved him. Watching the movie is an education as well as a profound experience.

I can't say I've personally seen or experienced a transformation as immediate and dramatic as that but I believe in such things. I believe that to be loved or to love someone changes the world; it actually becomes a different place. If Hollywood can imagine scenes like this why can't we? And if we can imagine it God said he can do it. Wouldn't it be a life-transforming experience to move up to a poor, jerking, contorted soul and begin the dance? Who knows what might happen? I wonder if I'm up to that? I wonder if I want to be up to it? It would probably be very costly. Hmmm.

# 6

## I KNOW SOMEONE

I know someone whose life is a mental and emotional maelstrom. She has no control over the raging winds of emotional and mental change that sweep over her. The best she can do is guzzle down the prescribed medicine and stay alive even while she inflicts on herself numerous little "suicides". She can't be depended on for any length of time to do the "normal" things; she knows she's "a burden" to her loving family and she's pretty well "useless" when it comes to congregational programs of outreach and edification.

She simply can't understand why God would keep her around. Why doesn't he just end her life and relieve her of terror and pain and the world of having to bear with her? She's filled with protest and tears and pleas for release and at other times with pleas for life rather than tortured existence.

But she cannot because she will not and will not because she cannot turn from God! In her lucid moments she reaffirms her trust in him!

She reminds me of a man I read about whose life was agony, whose pain was excruciating, whose confusion was complete and whose hot protest never ended from morning until night. Drunks sang songs about him, children mocked him, acquaintances avoided him and friends ladled out irrelevant teaching and advice. But would he quit; would he walk away from God? Not if the stars fell from heaven and the ground opened up and swallowed him whole!

He hated his existence, wished God would end it and yet, even more, he wanted the days back when he and God were friends and life proved it. No doubt there were those that looked at him and thought him useless and certainly some of his advisors thought him a positive blot on God's good name, a stumbling-block to other people. But when the entire story was told it was this man that God brought out into the light and gloried in. Job might have told God, "You know there were times when you made it hard for me to believe in you." If he had, God might have said, "That's interesting, for you always made it easy for me to believe in you."

# 7

## NOT ON THEIR WATCH

It's a great Story! There are no losers or useless among Christ's chosen. None at all! They're all on the walls keeping watch and playing their part. They come in different sizes, shapes, ages, degree of giftedness, particularity of giftedness, social status, physical and mental health—but they all serve!

They're not always "happy" because they're not always able to be "happy" due to their life's circumstances but it isn't only the happy people that serve His gracious purposes. People in the world might "go down" despite their presence in it, but they won't go down without their being on watch and just by their physical presence offering an alternative.

The walls they guard are not just the "church" walls. These "chosen in Christ" are not just "church patriots"—they're "cosmic patriots" (to borrow Chesterton's phrase). They maintain a presence in the world but they do it for the world! Their enemies are not flesh and blood as such; they are enemies of all that is an enemy of flesh and blood and all that insinuates itself into flesh and blood as a parasite and a destroyer of the human family.

These chosen ones have no sense of superiority; they are as sick and beaten-up as the peoples of the world around them. If you cut them they bleed, if you cheat them they feel betrayed, they weep at the graves of their dead ones and groan at a child that has gone astray or a marriage that has fallen apart. They have no personal charisma that the world should admire them but what they have (by God's good and sustaining grace) is a Story and a place in that Story.

Poor souls might go down to oblivion but they won't go down unnoticed or unattended—not on their watch!

# *8*

## A LETTER TO A VERY ILL FRIEND

It cannot be other than that all who love you and your loved ones would ask God for healing and health. That's how it should be. How could it be otherwise?

But as someone who has watched all of you now for a long time I'm more impressed by the health of your faith and faithfulness—you and your family. How pleasing it is to see such a network not only of affection and burden bearing but deep and unswerving trust. Though this speaks much about you and yours it says much about God—that you and yours judge him to be trustworthy even in the depths when you sometimes lose sight of emotional landmarks. How have you come to think this way of God? Who has grasped your hearts that you would say without apology—day after trying day—"If he does not heal me, still we will trust him!"—who brought you to such faith? He must be special indeed. He must have done some profound and lasting something that enables you all to experience what you experience and trust him still.

That a battle is being waged here in plain sight against disease, depression, weariness and disappointment is for all to see. But that's only a token of what is going on beyond, where the eye can't see and the taut nerves can't feel. It didn't matter that Job didn't know that he was fighting God's battle for him—it was true just the same. Cosmic and profound things were hanging in the balance. And it doesn't matter that you and yours think you're not in the Joban league; you are, and you too are fighting God's battle for him against all the forces of cynicism and darkness. Against all the voices and powers that say there is no true human faith, that God is loved only when he pours out blessings as bribes. Something bigger than a wrestle with disease and fear and pain is going on; this I believe.

I would wish that you and yours would be able—however difficult it is—for at least a part of a day, to focus not on the battle with the disease but on the truth that you are warring God's war for him and bearing witness to a frightened world of truth and hope and life beyond disease. I wish you might reflect on the grandeur of such an adventure and (as if the faith were not your own but someone else's that you feel free to admire) admire what is going on in your hearts while other things are going on within your body. I wish that you could rejoice and find strength in the very existence of your faith. We're all sure that God is glorious but part of the reason we believe that is because of what he does in people like you and yours. Take some of the energy you daily summon to resist the disease and focus on the glory of your faith and admire the girl (and the family) on whom God has risked his reputation.

genuinely, jim mcguiggan

[This young friend who had been very seriously ill for some years died not long after I wrote this to her.]

# 9

## LIFE IN STRANGE PLACES

Imagine looking down from a high place across the vast expanse of the Arabian Desert where stunted vegetation, wind-smoothed rock formations, scurrying reptiles, pitiless heat and dust were at home. Imagine seeing a nation and its herds down there, living, and even prospering, despite their hardships. Life in a strange place.

Paul, a prisoner (maybe in Rome but more likely in Caesarea—see the literature on the matter) writes to the Philippians (4:22) about "saints in Caesar's household". That's in Nero's household! That's life in a strange place.

Peter speaks to his Jewish brothers and sisters and sends the greeting of "she who is in Babylon, chosen together with you" (1 Peter 5:13). Whether he has in mind the ancient but now diminished and all-but-forgotten city of Babylon on the Euphrates or under a figure he means Rome—it's still life in a strange place.

See the old man with a body older than his years, now "as good as dead" and his long-barren wife (Abraham and Sarah) and remember that they became the parents of countless children. Life in a strange place.

I know there are people that don't believe this and I know that some of them can't believe it right now, for one reason or another, but God is always doing that, isn't he? In strange places he brings life into being.

In cruel homes we find gentle Christians. In homes awash with cynicism and criticism we find generous-hearted people who continue to believe that all wrongs will be righted and that the proper response to life is hope in God. Right alongside deeply entrenched bitterness and hardness we find people that give and forgive as if it were easy (though we all know it's very costly to them). Life in strange places.

I remember some years ago we finally felt compelled to surface our driveway. I had them spray it with weed-killer, then spread a million tons of gravel over it and follow that with thirty million tons of hot, sticky tar and gravel. Then I had them bring in a billion-ton steam-roller that rolled all that stuff flatter than a starfish. Goodbye weeds and dirt. I don't know how long it was after that that one day I stubbed my shoed-toe on a tiny mound in the middle of that driveway. I took a close look and there, peeping up out of a tiny hole, was a yellowy little sprout of some kind. Life in a strange place.

One day in all the graveyards of the world there's going to be a stirring.

# *10*

## AWAY FROM HOME

In Spielberg's E.T. the alien that is left behind when the spaceship leaves is befriended by a boy, who if it came to it, would give his life for the little creature. And what's more ET senses this and finds a deep pleasure, even joy, in the child's company. However brief the relationship it was one of those that blossomed immediately, as if it was meant to be. You might have seen such a thing or, if you've been very blessed, you might have experienced one like it. A lot depends on the persons involved, doesn't it? It seems some people can love a lifetime in only a few moments and others, poor souls, seem not to be able to commit to love even for a few moments even in a lifetime.

The child asks ET where he lives, pointing to a place on a world map and then to himself, indicating where he lived. That was his home and he asks ET where his home was. The little alien makes some balls float in the air to illustrate galaxies and then waddling to the window he points out into the night sky and with a heart-jerking and mournful tone he says, "Home." Several times in the movie we hear that mournful, missing-home tone as he sadly says, "Home."

I'm not now speaking of those whose lives are one prolonged crucifixion. Most of us have some pain and loss to bear even though we truly believe that all in all we have a good life. But however fine life is for us—if we're not hedonist to the core—don't we experience weariness sometimes? Some say they never do and I fully believe them and I'm glad for them; but for the rest of us, I suspect we get world-weary. Sometimes, however rarely, there comes the distant but definite longing just to lay down "the burden" of existing. Just to go to sleep—permanently! We can all, I'm sure, make a list of possible reasons for those feelings and I'm sure too that some of them would be on target.

It doesn't seem to matter that our finances are adequate, our family is loving and supportive and doing well. It doesn't seem to matter that we have a job that is satisfying in the various ways we think important or that our health is better than we have a right to expect. We're able to enjoy music, creation, friends, political freedom, the respect of our peers and the other things that make life sweet. And yet...here it comes...that sense of...ennui or weariness.

The boy was all to ET that he could be and he would have been more if he could—gladly! But for all his longing to please and satisfy him, he still sees ET waddle to the window, point into the night sky with that long bulbous finger and sadly say, "Home!"

And if it should be that every now and then when, despite your blessings and despite the fact that you know you are richly blessed, to feel an inner emptiness, don't deny it; acknowledge it. It might well be God nibbling at the edges of your mind, telling you that you were made for more than all you now have; that in truth you'll always be "homesick" away from God. It might well be that while gratefully enjoying what you have some night you should look into the heavens and hear yourself saying, "Home."

# 11

## WHICH GOD EXISTS?

"I for my part would much rather have men say of me that there never was a Plutarch at all, nor is now, than to say that Plutarch is a man inconstant, fickle, easily moved to anger, revengeful for trifling provocations, vexed at small things." That's what Plutarch said and doesn't it make moral and spiritual sense?

It isn't enough for us to affirm that God exists. In the final analysis it is of critical importance to say that the "God and Father of our Lord Jesus Christ" exists. That gives God a character and gives us personal reason to praise him and good reason to brag on him before the world. George Adam Smith was surely right when he said: "For the chief thing for individuals, as for nations, is not to believe that God reigns so much as to know what kind of God He is who reigns."

We're not interested in a god who's the cold conclusion of a rational syllogism or a villain like spiteful Zeus or some other mythical being. Though the God we worship must be altogether above us he must be of such a character that we can honour him.

When we call him "good" there must be something recognisably good about him or we couldn't praise him. The agnostic John Stuart Mill said that, and he was right.

The great news is that God is like Christ and in him is no unChristlikeness at all (compare John 14:7-9 and Hebrews 1:3). A God like that we are not only willing to worship, we can't keep ourselves from it and it is in that character that his greatest power lies. When you begin to worry about "eternal decrees" or where God is taking the world remember that the one true God is the God and Father of our Lord Jesus Christ. And if that's true, we're in good hands.

# 12

## HAMMERS AND SCALPELS

"Zophar the Naamathite enters upon the scene after Job had denied his guilt with a vehemence which seemed to demand a more direct rebuke from his listeners; but Zophar is hardly fitted to do it, for, with intellectual gifts of a high order, he has a bluntness of speech which will rouse the worst feelings in Job. He is just the man to take a hammer and hit a nail on the head, but the last person to do a delicate piece of moral surgery--probe a sensitive conscience, remove the source of irritation and tenderly bind up the wound." That's what Minos Devine said.

Many of us respect the Zophar types among us but very few have any real affection for them. There's always the thought nibbling at the edges of our minds that he might come after us one day and if he did we'd find it hard to bear. We like our critics to be gentle. In fact, we don't like our critics much at all. We could well live without them. I think it was Oscar Wilde who said he liked criticism of his work when it took the form of three hundred pages of closely reasoned and well argued adulation.

But like them or not we need them because some of us all the time and (I suppose) all of us some of the time will just not pay attention to people who "almost say something." If it is bitter medicine we must take then we ought to take it in one big spoonful—down the hatch, no sipping the foul-tasting but healing concoction. We will shout no hurrahs for blunt people like that that relish their work but we may live long enough to thank God for them, that someone had the courage to take us by the lapels and make us hear life or death, disease or health instruction.

I confess I lack that healthier capacity to confront. I must be forced into confronting or I tend to try to dodge the obligation. When it comes down to it I do it, you understand, but it's a serious challenge for me. I have a friend who is very good at it and can minister to people in that way without exulting in the pain it often generates in the person rebuked. There were times when someone I knew needed to be chastised and I was unable to do it that I enlisted my colleague's assistance (I can assure you it was all quite proper). It was most often because I was close to the person and was his or her chief source of affirmation. Sternness from me would have seemed to them to be a physical assault on their person and I couldn't do it. But they would have expected it from my friend so it wouldn't have been so traumatic and they would have given heed. At least this is how I excused myself and most of the time I believed I was doing what was best for them. But I had my moments of doubt, regarding myself as gutless and feeling guilty as well.

Then I read Paul Tournier, the famous European psychologist, a man I respected deeply, confessing the very same thing. He too had a colleague whose temperament and giftedness enabled him to speak very sternly without being "over the top" and Tournier would call on him for assistance. That consoled and assured me. It might have meant that there were two gutless people in the world but while I could think that of me I couldn't think it of Tournier. Even as I express these thoughts I think how self-serving my "scheming" might have been since it meant that Jim (me) was protecting himself ("Jim is such a gentle person, isn't he?" they would say of me). And they might have thought of my friend as a hard man ("—— is always telling someone off, isn't he?"). But I'm willing to live with the inner tension because I think God uses our differing temperaments for different jobs. Maybe even in the spiritual and emotional we should know not to use a scalpel to open a packing case or a sledgehammer to crack a nut.

*A know-it-all is a bore and often arrogant but the mealy-mouthed is tedious and often gutless*

# 13

## LEAVE NO DOUBT

We have to live with doubt not only because we lack sufficient information to come to a final conclusion about many things but also because we're limited in our ability to process information and relate to life's situations. That's part of the human condition even for good and wise and caring people so we shouldn't grovel in shame over it even though at times, depending on what's at stake, we're deeply saddened that we don't know how best to help or respond.

But beyond that, there are those who tell us that we should profess uncertainty always in all circumstances about all things. This is nonsense as well as impossible. G.K Chesterton protested against that spurious humility when he looked around him and surmised that one of these days we're going to be so humble that we'll doubt that two plus two equal four.

To know something is not to know everything but it's not to know nothing either! We can't be sure of everything but it's nonsense to say we can be sure of nothing! Caution and reserving judgement is healthy but too much "humility" is possible and saturating our speech on just about everything with phrases like, "of course, on the other hand" is a mental/social disease.

A know-it-all is a bore and often arrogant but the mealy-mouthed is tedious and often gutless

In a movie an American football coach is earnestly calling his team to wholehearted commitment to the game at hand and urges them to make it clear to their opponents that they had come out to engage in war, so to speak. His final word of instruction is: "Leave no doubt!"

Not everything that Christians believe is absolutely certain or clear but some things are and in these matters Christians should leave no doubt!

"There is one true God and it is the God that has revealed himself to us in and as Jesus Christ and we're his followers!" Of that the Christian should leave no doubt.

Others don't believe that and for one reason or another, or for many reasons, they cannot yet believe it; but that's not to the point. These people aren't Christians and they don't profess to be.

Christians are to leave no doubt!

They're not to apologise or to waver or to mumble; they're not to equivocate! They're not to suggest or imply or hint or guess or settle for "the preponderance of the evidence". In this matter they're not to act uncertain or to dither or vacillate

They're to leave no doubt!

They may be wrong but if they're wrong they aren't a little wrong, they're profoundly wrong! They're not to have one eye on the biblical witness and one eye on the latest poll or what book's in the best-seller list. They're not to wring their hands or anguish in the night about what governments or courts will decide about how they can or must express their faith. They're not to have one foot in the door of the church and the other dragging just in case they feel the need to beat a sheepish retreat; half-heartedness in this area is not permissible. They have no back doors to slip out of, no lawyer-like covering of their tracks to fall back on and if they're wrong then of all the people in the world they're the most pathetic.

Christians are to leave no doubt!

If they discovered their faith is false their dismay should be written all over them! They should be devastated and red-faced. They should make it known that if Jesus Christ is a fraud or a myth or if he was demented or misunderstood—if anything like that is true the Christians should make it known that their entire world has collapsed around them and that they've been hoodwinked in no uncertain manner.

Christians have no right to be insolent or scornful of others but neither do they have any grounds to beat around the bush or be evasive. We're not gingerly "testing the Christian waters". Our wholehearted confession is that Jesus is Lord and in him the one true God has unveiled himself and his eternal intentions regarding the human family.

This we believe and Christians should leave no doubt!

*And as we lie in our silent graves with no earthly help that will make any difference, paralyzed by a crushing hopelessness, we hear the whisper of the wind; and the word of God comes to us again through a nation that was dead in sin and beyond all human help.*

# 14

## THE WIND OF THE SPIRIT

Many of us go through spiritually depressed periods that feel like near-death experiences. On advice, we read the rich biblical texts that have helped so many others, yet our hearts remain as cheerless and lifeless as a cold fireplace. We try all the spiritual tonics, speak to all the wise people, do all the spiritual aerobics, read all the books on the spiritual disciplines, and try the "seven steps" offered by the well-known authors — all to no avail. Our depression deepens, and despair begins to knock on the doors of our hearts.

All those cures are supposed to work! They appear to have worked for other people and churches, why not us? That they haven't worked for us is a matter of real concern if we are serious about having a relationship with God that pleases rather than grieves him, one that involves our giving as well as receiving. But our prayers and promises — our vows, sworn in blood-red earnestness that we'd be better, speak better, do better, and think better — have all come to nothing. The vows were sincere — at least we thought they were — and they were made in agony. But when the passion cools, we feel that "the summer is gone and we are not saved." Despair or near despair sets in. And why wouldn't it? We share the poet's distress:

*Weary of passions unsubdued,*
*Weary of vows in vain renewed,*
*Of forms without the power,*
*Of prayers, and hopes, complaints, and groans,*

*My fainting soul in silence owns*
*I can hold out no more.*

And the words of the sufferer become ours, "My God, my God, why have you forsaken me? Why are you so far from saving me, so far from the words of my groaning?" (Psalm 22:1)

And in our hearts, they aren't words snarled in bitterness — they're weary and disappointed rather than angry, because with our track record we can blame no one but ourselves. Still... still... we were hoping that God in his mercy would take sides with us against ourselves and deliver us for his own name's sake.

"O my God, I cry out by day, but you do not answer, by night, and am not silent." (Psalm 22:2) And as we complain, we're perplexed, because the God to whom we make our appeal has a reputation as a deliverer: "Yet you are enthroned as the Holy One; you are the praise of Israel. In you our fathers put their trust; they trusted and you delivered them. They cried to you and were saved; in you they trusted and were not disappointed." (Psalm 22:3-5)

*Wonderful stories. Salvation stories. True stories. But all the more distressing because they are true. Others called and were saved. We call and instead of rescue we continue to see ourselves as worms, and our "enemies" mock us even though we throw ourselves on God for deliverance. (Psalm 22:6)*

So we lie down, exhausted, having despaired of ourselves and feeling that God must have despaired of us also. And as we lie in our silent graves with no earthly help that will make any difference, paralyzed by a crushing hopelessness, we hear the whisper of the wind; and the word of God comes to us again through a nation that was dead in sin and beyond all human help.

As a nation they had tried everything to stave off the death they richly deserved. They paid tribute until they were broke, made treaties with foreign powers, and sent ambassadors north, south, east, and west. They fortified cities and studied the ways of war. They even tried religion — they built altars and prayed. But there was no salvation in any of their efforts. They were all just new ways of speeding the death process, and they ended up in a national grave. (Ezekiel 37:1-14)

Their bones were more than dry; they were "very dry." And there weren't only a few of them — the valley, like one giant coffin, was choked with them. The prophet spoke, and bone came together with bone; but there was no life — there was only a huge ravine full of skeletons. Sinews and flesh wound themselves around the bones, but there was no life — only a mighty gorge filled with corpses, an eerie, silent valley of corpses! Well, not absolutely silent. There was the wind. The man was told to speak the word of God to the wind, and the wind became the Spirit of God entering those lifeless figures — just as on the day of creation —and they were filled with life and stood on their feet, a mighty army. A nation alive from the dead!

And hearing their story, we're persuaded to trust again —or at least not to not trust again. At this very moment, we may feel a sense of fatigue and despair, but it's not the end of the story. God —and may it please him to be soon —will give us reason to rejoice as life courses through us, delivering us from one enemy after another. One day we'll assemble to worship and feel compelled to turn to fellow-worshipers and speak of our deliverance. In the strength and joy of the Spirit of God, we'll dismiss depression's view of sadder days and say with the psalmist:

*He has not despised or disdained*
*the suffering of the afflicted one;*
*he has not hidden his face from him*
*but has listened to his cry for help.*

And we, as our forefathers did, will enthrone God as the Holy One and the praise of our hearts. From him will come the theme of our praise in the great assembly, (Psalm 22:25) and our story will be told as one of deliverance to children not born and people will trust because we were delivered (22:30-31).

And what is true of individuals can be true of whole congregations, and what is true of congregations can be true of cities and nations! What is true for others can be true for you. What is true for you can be true for me. Weep if you must, and tell him your poor heart's breaking —but trust, wait, and listen for the wind!

# 15

## THE TYRANT'S SULK

King Ahab owned half the country for pity's sake. Summer houses here, autumn houses there and winter palaces elsewhere. What more could he want? He wanted Naboth's vineyard! 1 Kings 21:1-4. He saw it, made more than a fair offer for it but Naboth couldn't part with it, didn't want to part with it and so he wouldn't part with it.

And what did the king do? The land baron went home to his palace, to his bed and there he lay in a royal sulk with a huge bottom lip. "Leave me alone. Don't want any supper!" Nothing he possessed—list what he had why don't you?—nothing he possessed made him happy; if he couldn't have that one little piece of property next door he couldn't enjoy anything he had. The respect of his troops couldn't keep him out of bed. The praise of the architects and builders who were impressed with his marvellous building achievements couldn't deliver him from that huge pout. The text tells us he lies with his face to the wall—poor thing, bad ole Naboth won't sell him his garden so nothing else matters. *"Yes, yes, I'm blessed beyond imagining but what good are the blessings? What does it matter that a host of people please me and want to continue to please me? What they do and think isn't enough to keep me from being unhappy."*

We don't begrudge Ahab his wanting Naboth's vineyard but because he can't get it he runs home to his bed and lies there pouting with his face to the wall—in a palace?

If a tragedy occurred to one of my dearest I'd be gutted even though much remained a source of rejoicing. If you have five children you truly love and in some tragedy of some kind—whether in death or some other way—you lose one, your pain is not to be trifled with; it's too deep for that! It doesn't help a lot when good friends remind you that you still have plenty to be thankful for. Five beloved children minus one doesn't = plenty. Do you think this is the kind of thing I'm thinking about when I talk about Ahab? No, that's not what I have in mind. We mustn't hurry people out of their grief even though in wise love we'll nurture them toward better emotional health.

No, I'm thinking of that super-sensitivity that sees every refusal as a personal insult; that childish tendency to childish tantrums, with or without the visible signs of tantrum; that juvenile attitude that uses the pout as the lever to move a home or a church out of a happy path. I'm talking about that make-up that has to have everything its own way or the nearest and dearest will pay! I'm talking about a heart that mustn't be confronted or a week-long silent treatment begins. There's no physical violence but the dread that some families live in lest they say the wrong thing or don't say the right thing sometimes seems worse than physical abuse. C.S Lewis said you can only commit murder a relatively few times but you can cripple and emotionally wound ceaselessly, and all around you, with that sullen, grieving, dampening spirit that soaks into everyone within reach.

And you'll have noticed that it's the persons that give most to these tyrants that suffer most from them. Strangers and acquaintances would walk away from them but their loved ones bend over backwards to please.

In homes the family members walk around whispering and suppressing simple ordinary activities in case they disturb the sulking monarch. Televisions must be turned down too low for comfort, doors must be closed gently, and nobody is to laugh in case his /her majesty thinks his /her colossal sulk is going unnoticed.

In congregations these tyrants must be visited often and reassured sickeningly often that their views are taken with the utmost seriousness even if the congregational flow can't be turned out of it channels.

In God's name, grow up and get over it!

*And it isn't hard to understand that at times we'll say, "That makes no sense!" And those words are not far removed (only in intensity are they different) from, "Meaningless! Meaningless! Absolutely meaningless!"*

# 16

## MEANINGLESS! MEANINGLESS!

I might have told you about the tall, glossy-haired kid (late twenties) with the little black and white television set that (as he put it) "gets four channels really good." Maybe I told you that he lived next door to Ethel and me a while back. He was the kid with the big brown eyes, one of them that wasn't quite centred, yeah the kid with the dirty and shabby and ill-fitting clothes, jobless, who'd been on and off drugs and booze and done some time in prison. That's him—the one that hanged himself and wasn't discovered for two or three days. Did I tell you that when I first went in to see him he told me he was reading his Bible? Yep! Showed it to me, a little blue, small-print hard-backed Bible. And his grubby notebook, in which he had scribbled a lot of notes with his ballpoint pen. Did I tell you it was Ecclesiastes he was reading? Yeah, that was it. You remember how that book opens, don't you?

"Meaningless! Meaningless! Utterly meaningless! Everything is meaningless!" How'd a book like that ever get into the Bible? The writer goes to make his point by describing what he took to be the mindless repetition of the world around us (Ecclesiastes 1:3-11). He saw the sun rising and setting, rising and setting, rising and setting, rivers emptying into the seas and then being replenished, emptying and being replenished. And he groans out the words.

I hear people talking like that when they're very depressed. Sometimes the depression is enduring and clinical, sometimes it's the reaction to a tragedy that simply takes out of them the desire to live even while they go on living. It's all perfectly understandable. In cases like these the people groan about life's pointlessness but not all of them mean it—it's pain and mental muddle joining forces. They're blessed with a "master story" that remains intact even in the depths of feelings of despair.

There's reason to believe that the teacher in Ecclesiastes is speaking out of the depths of depression and for the most part his profoundly soured view of existence blots out any interpretation of life that might free his spirit. So we get the savagely dull groan, "Meaningless! Utterly meaningless! Everything is meaningless!"

Jesus was never without his "master story" and whatever he saw pointed away from despair. In Matthew 5:43-48 he's teaching his disciples the nature of the love of God and how they should live in God's image. He saw the sun rise and set, rise and set, rise and set and his response was, "Isn't the Holy Father wonderful and generous?!" He saw the rivers empty and be replenished by rain, emptied and replenished, emptied and replenished and he said, "Isn't the Holy Father ceaselessly gracious?!" He went on to say that God makes the sun to shine and the rain to fall on the fields of those who care nothing for him. His response to the rhythms of nature was the opposite to that of Qoheleth, "the teacher," in that strange OT book.

I don't say it's easy to think and react the way Jesus Christ did—I only say there are solid grounds for doing it since it's how he responded. There's no denying that there's a God-denying appearance to the world. Natural "laws" pay no mind though you're gentle or your kind; they crush the innocent and the righteous along with the wicked. Evil people enjoy success and their fields produce, their families thrive and their businesses flourish. Surely God should love only those that love him (and us)—but he won't do that.

And it isn't hard to understand that at times we'll say, "That makes no sense!" And those words are not far removed (only in intensity are they different) from, "Meaningless! Meaningless! Absolutely meaningless!"

Qoheleth looked at some things, we look at other things and together we groan, "Pointless!" Jesus Christ looks at them all, then at us, and says, "Trust me, it's the very opposite. There is meaning and point! Trust me, and if you do, one day you'll understand and you won't be able to contain your joy. Trust me, I know what I'm talking about; and I never lie."

*And that's a funny thing, when you come to think of it. We're just babies making up a game, if you're right. But four babies playing a game can make a play-world which licks your real world hollow. That's why I'm going to stand by the play-world. I'm on Aslan's side even if there isn't any Aslan to lead it. I'm going to live as like a Narnian as ever I can even if there isn't any Narnia.*

# 17

## PUDDLEGLUM

Eustace, Jill and Puddleglum, the Marsh-wiggle, had travelled far together on an assignment from Aslan, C. S Lewis tells us and now they find themselves in the Underland and in the presence of the witch-queen of that gloomy domain. They had found Prince Rilian and would have been pleased to go home immediately but it wasn't that simple. "Home"? Where was that? The witch-queen had filled their hungry bellies and with sweet words she assured them that her dark and gloomy world was all there was. So she said, as she strummed her hypnotic music and threw a strange powder on the fire. The music and the aroma were stealing the memories and so were stealing the minds of the adventurers. There is no other world, there is no Narnia, there is no great lion called Aslan-—those are all dreams, figments of the imagination that a good dose of realism would cure. But great truths are stubborn things and Puddleglum was no wild dreamer. He knew the difference between gloom and pointlessness and knew how shabby the life the witch-queen of gloom, in here good Freudian fashion, was offering compared with a world he knew was real. He speaks for a host when he rises against the great seducer:

"One word, Ma'am," he said, coming back from the fire; limping because of the pain. "One word. All you've been saying is quite right, I shouldn't wonder. I'm a chap who always liked to know the worst and then put the best face I can on it. So I won't deny any of what you said. But there's one thing more to be said, even so. Suppose we have only dreamed, or made up, all those things— trees and grass and sun and moon and stars and Aslan himself. Suppose we have. Then all I can say is that, in that case, the made-up things seem a good deal more important than the real ones. Suppose this black pit of a kingdom of yours is the only world. Well, it strikes me as a pretty poor one. And that's a funny thing, when you come to think of it. We're just babies making up a game, if you're right. But four babies playing a game can make a play-world which licks your real world hollow. That's why I'm going to stand by the play-world. I'm on Aslan's side even if there isn't any Aslan to lead it. I'm going to live as like a Narnian as ever I can even if there isn't any Narnia. So, thanking you kindly for our supper, if these two gentlemen and the young lady are ready, we're leaving your court at once and setting out in the dark to spend our lives looking for the Overland. Not that our lives will be very long, I should think; but that's a small loss if the world's as dull a place as you say."

Paul was realist enough to believe that if Christ hadn't risen from the dead the Christian faith is false and the Christians were more pathetic than any others in the world. But he knew! Christ had risen. So without conceding anything, we'd say with Puddleglum that the world non-believers think is wishful nonsense is a better world and true to the best in humanity than the gloomy existence of which the atheist, H. J Blackham, "It's too bad to be true!" He thought the greatest argument against unbelief was, "Its pointlessness…It's too bad to be true." Christians, with Puddleglum, would sort of say about the Christian faith, "It's too good not to be true."

# 18

## THE GOSPEL AND THE UNLUCKY

The good news is about God keeping his commitment to humanity despite humanity's rebellion and sinfulness. He demonstrates and proclaims his faithfulness finally and completely in the person and work of Jesus Christ. So say the scriptures.

But what if you're born and raised in a part of the world where that gospel is not known? Hmmm, that's tough luck!

So, that's it? God is faithful and shows it in Christ who goes to the cross, triumphs over death and lives to bless us all but if you aren't lucky enough to hear it you're damned? For tens of millions down the years the cross has been neutralized by bad luck? Since saving faith comes by the gospel and some people aren't lucky enough to hear it they lose out? They get one chance to sin and be damned but no chance to be saved?

Some Calvinist types tell us that such people were ordained to damnation and that's why they don't get to hear. In some ways that's worse than "bad luck" it's "bad fate". It's bad luck as well, in the sense that those people weren't part of the group God decided he'd save. They tell us that God is Father to every human but that he made millions of his children for no other reason that to show his glory by damning them eternally.

Some Arminian types blame the loss of multiplied millions on lazy Christians who won't spread the message. These "lazy" Christians with no missionary heart ceaselessly tell their fellow-saved ones that they are indeed saved and that they should be ecstatic about it; but they can't be bothered to tell the unsaved how to be saved. Some shrewd Arminian types cover their backs, however, by telling us that God must know they wouldn't obey anyway, even if they heard the gospel. So he doesn't get it to them. If he foresaw that they would obey, God would see to it that they heard. I suppose that'll satisfy some people. Just the same, it leaves us with an uneasy feeling that that proposal is a bit too convenient. The bottom line is that all those who die untold deserve to die untold. Nice easy way to sidestep Matthew 28:18-20. Then again, maybe it's neither nice nor easy. Maybe Matthew 28:18-20 is not the kind of word we can sidestep. Whatever we make of all that, the untold are still left untold and, we're assured, they're as lost as Judas.

It looks like the untold have it tough all the way round. On the one view if you're one of the untold you've been ordained to damnation and on the other if you die untold you wouldn't have believed anyway so you weren't told. On the one view you weren't told because God didn't want you told and on the other you weren't told because the saved were too busy telling each other that at least they were saved. The one thing that's certain is that the untold are damned. However you look at it, that's unlucky—gospel or no gospel.

I care little for the conversations I sometimes find running through my mind; conversations about what could happen when an untold one arrives at judgement. A Calvinistic God dialogues with an untold sinner.

"It's everlasting punishment for you."

"Well, I'm a sinner and I deserve it I guess. And who are those people over there that look so fine and are alive with life?"

"They are the heirs of glory, my children whom I've freely forgiven."

"I see, they're your sinful children just like me?"

"Yes."

"How come I didn't end up as part of that group? Was I worse than them?"

"Oh no, it has nothing to do with who's good or bad or better or worse. I decided who I'd save and who I'd damn eternally before I ever created any of my children. So it has nothing to do with your choice or theirs.

"Ah, I see, so it's eternal life or eternal destruction based simply and solely on a decision you made about each one of us before ever we came along?

"Now, you've got it."

"I know I can't deny my sin any more than those saved ones can deny theirs, but how come you didn't choose me to be part of that saved group?

"It's simple: I didn't want you and I wanted them."

"Oh! I see. Um...okay then."

"You understand?"

"I understand your words. I don't understand that you would create me as one of your children but that you wouldn't want me."

"Ah, yes, but that's not for you to question my child. That's one of the mysteries that's beyond little puny humans."

"Obviously! So where do I go to be eternally destroyed?"

"Follow that line of multiplied millions. There are a lot of you I didn't want."

But that's not the only conversation that I imagine; there's this little beauty. An Arminian God dialogues with an untold sinner.

God says: "It's eternal punishment for you."

"I hate that. I wish there had been a way out of this mess I made."

"There was a way! I sent my Son to save you by redeeming you but you didn't accept him."

"I didn't accept him? I never even heard about him!"

"Well, that's not my fault. I did my part in sending Christ and giving the gospel to my elect."

"And where are they?"

"They're busy right now. They're telling one another how gracious I am. And they're telling each other that they can be certain they're saved so they ought to enjoy themselves."

"I see, that's their job; to keep telling each other that you have saved them?"

"Well, yes, but they're supposed to tell people like you that you can be saved as well."

"But they didn't tell me."

"Yes, that's true, and they should have done it. Still, they're weak and sinful and I forgive them for that."

"Hmmm. So they're weak and sinful like me. But they're in and I'm out because they heard and I didn't?"

"Actually, you're not lost because you didn't hear. You're lost because you sinned."

"But they sinned just like me and they're not lost."

"Yes, but they turned to me in Jesus Christ when they heard the gospel."

"How come they got to hear the gospel? Were they just lucky?"

"No, I provide the gospel to those who hear so they can be saved."

"Did you want me saved?"

"Yes."

"Then why didn't you provide it for me?"

"I bring it to the lost through the elect."

"But you didn't bring it to me through the elect."

"Yes, but they are the ones who fell down on the job."

"So, you truly wanted me to hear it, they didn't tell me and I'm about to experience eternal punishment?"

"That's about it."

"But in the end, is it not true that you didn't really provide all I need to be saved from my sin? See, I had understood that you provided all that was needed for sinners like me to get saved and yet I wasn't offered the gospel without which sinners can't be saved."

"Well, that's true but you can't blame me for the sins of the elect."

"I get one chance to sin and be damned and not one chance to be saved while those people over there who are all glorious and happy with life got countless chances to be saved? It doesn't seem fair but more to the point it doesn't seem to fit the Story I've just been hearing."

"You talk like I owe you something. I don't owe you anything."

"I suppose that's true, but then you don't owe anybody anything. I didn't think this gospel was about you owing us. I thought it was about your vast generosity and grace."

"Well...it is and I really wanted you to be saved."

"So how come I'm about to suffer eternal destruction from your presence?"

"Hmmm...you're just unlucky I guess."

[And those are the only options? Bad luck or what Calvin called that "horrible decree"? I don't believe that for a moment!]

*Only the word "resurrection" makes Death grow pale and only the reality of that word turns Death into a vapor that will finally vanish as if it had never been.*

# 19

## DIALOGUE WITH DEATH

Is victory over death always sweet? Always! Though for some poor souls, wrestling in agony and too high strung, life is no prize to be cherished and death no enemy to be conquered. A host of our fellow-humans lie wishing for death, sometimes even begging for it and asking those that love them to wrench their lives from them. But it's only the ill and those for whom life is indeed a crushing weight and utterly without discernible purpose—it's only people like these that beg to be freed once and for all from the experience of living. (I grant that sometimes they're made to feel that they are burdens on those that "love" them and that dying is the only decent thing to do.) All this is understandable and those that say they don't grasp the reason for their fevered request should keep their mouths firmly shut about matters in this area. An iron horse would have enough feeling to have some grasp of a situation like that! Those for whom life is better than just tolerable and those for whom life is a glorious dance—these have no wish to die. And so it should be.

But victory over death is truly gained in and through resurrection. To win over death would have to mean more than surviving serious surgery or overcoming a major disease. For later, death would return and—whatever some silly people think—it will grasp them and take them with it to the "realm" of the dead. Only the word "resurrection" makes Death grow pale and only the reality of that word turns Death into a vapor that will finally vanish as if it had never been.

George Herbert knew what he was talking about. Here in one of his poems is his brief dialogue with death.

*Christian: Alas, poor Death, where is thy glorie?*
*Where is thy famous force, thy ancient sting?*
*Death: Alas poore mortal, void of storie,*
*Go spell and read how I have kill'd thy King.*
*Christian: Poor Death! And who was hurt thereby?*
*Thy curse being laid on him, makes thee accurst.*
*Death: Let losers talk: yet thou shalt die;*
*These arms shall crush thee.*
*Christian: Spare not, do thy worst, I shall be one day*
*better than before:*
*Thou so much worse, that you shalt be no more.*

But that vibrant and glorious hope is only for those embraced in the redeeming work of the Death Killer. This galvanising truth is not the pathetic self-assuring thing offered by Hollywood movies, where the amoral or half-decent or self-sufficient have nothing to fear in death. There is everything to fear in Death for those that cheapened life and expelled from it any thought of God or the gospel. This promise of full and immortal life is always and only given as a gift in and through Jesus Christ. Hollywood lies when it says: "You have nothing to worry about because you have within you what it takes to beat death. The other side is a continuation of the partying you have come to know and love so well."

And so, are we to settle for misery now in hope of a vibrant life in the future? I'll grant that some believers are such misery-bound moaners that they shame the promises of scripture. And I'm well aware that hosts of believers have lived tortured lives of deeper level pain and loneliness; but ignoring the extremes, there's more life in the weakest believer, more adventure and engagement with life, than in the masses of the beautiful bed-hopping people or the disco addicts that whirl like dervishes.

We watch the heroes in the Lord of the Rings as they battle their way through pain and loss and fear and uncertainty, but they do it with a stubborn refusal to bend to the enemy. We watch them, and it isn't their misery that we're taken with—it's their mission. Fiction or no, we wish them well, admire their bravery, we wish to be like them and we rise to our feet inside to applaud their victory. And after that we should go back to our discos, booze, drugs, another adrenalin-rush with the trivia that we call life? Well, some will.

We believers believe in life before death! No one enjoys a well-cooked steak—if a steak is to be had—more than a free believer does! No one takes more pleasure than a free Christian when biting into a crisp apple or drinking a clear cold glass of clean water, or making passionate love to a husband or wife, or wrestling with kids and grandkids, or camping or trekking or climbing or the smell of fresh-baked bread or careering down a rushing river in a tiny raft—no one! Not any one! And these blessings taste better and are more pleasant because the believer knows they are part of the proof of something more wonderful than all these. World! You have nothing on us. We outlive you even if we out-suffer you. We outlive you, even now, because we have come to know the Death Killer and even now we sense the beginnings of immortality.

*One of these days JB's teacher will say to all the loyal and blessed ones, "Well done, good and faithful servant, share in the joy of your Lord."*

# *20*

## GOOD AND FAITHFUL SERVANT

JB Whitman was a friend of mine. He was well read, passionate about Christ and the gospel and severe in his appraisal of messages that undermined that gospel. He was one of those that combined kindness with honesty and gentleness with forthrightness and that seems to be a rare ability. Because he was that way and because I knew he was I couldn't very well debate his qualifications when he responded to one of my messages when I visited the assembly of which he was one of the shepherds.

I'm not much of a speaker and I know it. I tend to ramble too much and have real difficulty in getting from A to B to C without numerous little diversions. I admire those that know where they're going, how to get there and who stick to the path. I oscillate between an emotional striptease and serious "bookishness". As a consequence I very often get in the way of the gospel I wish to present. That Sunday (though it may have been Wednesday) I felt that I had the usual wrestle but when I was done JB came and with what seemed to be deep-seated pleasure he said to me, "Well done, good and faithful servant." It wasn't just what he said that made the moment memorable for me; it was the quiet and thoughtful and pleased way he said it. Still, what he said gave me a lift I've never lost sight of and it made me want to do what he was sure I had done on that occasion. He thought I had been true to the gospel. (It might be vanity in me that leads me to mention this; on the other hand it might me that I feel the need of such assurance that I can't keep it in.)

This incident came to mind a while ago when a friend of mine completed a little series of meetings not far from here (and I didn't get to one of them). He came to eat with us and I asked him how he had worked with the messages he had agreed to bring. When he was done and without thinking of what I should say, I said "Well done, good and faithful servant." That was how his report and summary had made me feel about what he had done. It was only after he was gone I made all the connections with that moment and that precious moment with JB. I was pleased to be able to say to my friend that he had done well and was a good and faithful servant because that's what his summary had made me think. But it was in saying it to my friend that JB's word to me became even more precious. What I had said to John was a profoundly lovely thing; he had honoured himself in being faithful and the loveliest thing I could respond with was that truthful word. It was then—additionally—that I realised the great honor JB had bestowed on me and it meant that at least on that occasion I had done something worthwhile, I had been faithful to Jesus and his gospel.

One of these days JB's teacher will say to all the loyal and blessed ones, "Well done, good and faithful servant, share in the joy of your Lord."

Mmmm, love the very thought of that!

# *21*

## DR. JEKYLL & MR. HYDE

There are still a few around. They so talk about God that you'd think he was a Robert Louis Stevenson character. You remember, the devoted and kind doctor, Dr. Jekyll who took the drug and found he had an inner Mr. Hyde. Some people talk about God, of Christ and his cross, as if God in holiness could hardly wait to damn humanity and yet he gives his Son to deliver us. The notion that God's holiness means he's eager to damn sinners is sheer nonsense! "For God did not send his Son into the world to condemn the world but that the world through him might be saved." (John 3:17) Rather than provoking him to obliterate us completely, our awful sin provoked the Holy Father to mount a rescue operation so that he might remain faithful to his eternal commitment to his creation.

It's right to denounce sin and even more right to live it down in righteousness; but there's little point in our speaking or acting as though we took it more seriously than God does. We're not to fraternise with sin or be on friendly terms with the world but we mustn't pretend that our opposition to it is greater than God's. His opposition to sin is pitiless and ceaseless, but it's combined with a relentless love for sinners.

The cross of Jesus did not bribe God to adopt a forgiving mood—it was the expression of his eternal love.

The cross of Jesus did not buy grace from God—it was the unveiling of an eternally gracious God.

The cross of Jesus didn't persuade an unwilling God to come to our rescue—it was the final demonstration that God had indeed already moved that way.

Understandably we want God to crush impenitent unrighteousness; but one reason we're eager for that is because we don't have his capacity for endurance. We feel pain too keenly and are easily frustrated when our godly enterprises are thwarted by sinners. Our love pools are too shallow and when sinners come to drink of them too frequently they dry up; but, after all, we're only humans, only weak and sinful humans. God does not hold us responsible for not being God!

Just the same, in our anxiety to have the sinners and their sin destroyed we mustn't resent God for being the God he is; one who is not willing that any should perish!

# 22

## JESUS CHRIST AND CAMELOT

Tennyson tells us that King Arthur established the order of the Round Table; a table without a head or foot, where all were equal in their commitment to justice for all and might for right. His dream drew knights from all over England and Europe and the effects of it were felt all over the land; women could walk out in the evening alone without worry, doors were left unlocked, the roads were cleared of robbers and tyrants were disestablished but just when things were flourishing, the greatest knight of them all, Lancelot, set his eye on the Guinevere and she on him. The wickedness became known and Lancelot rode away only to return when he heard that the knights had demanded that Guinevere be tried for treason. She was tried and condemned to death but Lancelot came and rescued her and carried her off to France where she entered a convent. The knights and Arthur raged and for a while there was nothing but inflamed pride and vengeance in their hearts and so they sailed to France and prepared for war against Lancelot and his forces.

Arthur is broken-hearted and dispirited. The dream had failed, the purpose had died. The great sin of Guinevere and Lancelot had also exposed the underlying son of all of them when vengeance and bitterness reigned and offended pride had proved stronger than brotherhood and forgiveness.

In the musical adaptation the king is putting on his armour in the dawn of the day of battle when he hears a rustling in the bush; it was a boy about twelve who had stowed away on one of the ships—to kill the enemy and be a knight, he said. Arthur wanted to know why he would want to be part of an extinct fellowship. Had he ever met a knight, was his father a knight or had his mother been rescued by a knight? The answer to all these questions was no, so what did he know of knights? Only the stories he had heard, the boy said and when the king asked him what stories he spoke of justice for all, the round table and might used in the service of right. As the boy spoke the king was mouthing with him the words.

Stories! The story of the dream had kept the dream alive. The stories of righteousness and justice for all kept the vision alive in the heart of a boy who'd never even seen a knight. The deeply depressed king has gained new heart and knights the boy Sir Tom of Warwick with a commission to go home and grow old telling the story of the meaning of Camelot. Part of his instruction was this:

*Every evening from December to December*
*Before you fall asleep upon your cot*
*Think back on all the tales that you remember*
*Of Camelot.*
*Ask everyone if he has heard the story*
*And tell it loud and clear if he has not*
*Don't let it be forgot*
*That once there was a spot*
*For one bright shining moment*
*That was known as Camelot.*

At that moment an aide comes to remind the king that they have a battle to fight and win but the king, all smiles and optimism, assures his companion that their victory already stands before them in the heart of a boy who cherishes the story and what it means and who will tell it everywhere he goes. That being the case, what happens at the approaching battle is now irrelevant.

The massive truth on which all great fiction is built is that God's great purpose for the human family was and is accomplished in and through Jesus Christ and that it is God's wisdom by the foolishness of a preached message—a Story—to redeem the world (1 Corinthians 1:21). The victory has already been won by Jesus Christ and in his body, the Church, each new generation hears the Story—the message about God's dream and purpose that cannot be thwarted.

In ultimate truth, the world is saved not by science or philosophy or political reform however needful these are and no matter how true it is that these are instruments of God at his pleasure. The human family is saved and all things in heaven and on earth are reconciled to God and find their ultimate state of blessing in him about whom the Story is told.

The very existence of the Christian faith defies the world and is part of the ongoing proof that Jesus Christ has indeed conquered the world (1 John 5:4-5).

*The awful evil that pervades our world sometimes shocks us into a fear-filled silence. It is astonishing how perverse and indifferent we can be something else astonishes us sometimes: How is it that anyone in a world like this believes in the Lord Jesus? How does he do that?*

# 23

## A JOYFUL AND ADEQUATE JESUS

It was to Jesus in Matthew 15:21-28 that a woman of faith said something like: "I'm not asking for the children's food; don't want them to be neglected. I'll settle for the scraps. Your crumbs are all I need for they're more than a full-sized meal."

A text says, "As many as touched him were made perfectly whole." Someone I can't trace said this, "His way through the world had something of the character of a triumphal procession of the powers of life and gladness for where He came, people who scarcely knew by what name to call Him, hailed Him as one who was clearly adequate for His chosen task of helping men."

It's right to see sin as the life-sucking parasite that it is and we must see the sombre side of the business of destroying it. It's vitally important, however, for us to see the cure as a matter of supreme joy, something to celebrate, something to smile, even dance, about. Whoever is killing this killer must surely be rejoicing, must surely find satisfaction and profound pleasure and if in the hospital the doctors came to us, with relief on their faces, to tell us that we had turned the corner and that the devourer was dying, would we not grin?

The analogy, though limited, is a good one and we must surely see Jesus as going through the world with joy in his heart and a smile on his young face. This is life he is dispensing, health he is handing out, as he destroys the dominion of sin and sets the prisoners free and heals the diseased.

When the disciples came and told him that the evil powers were subject to them because of his name we're told that Jesus rejoiced! Did he laugh out loud? I don't know but it wouldn't surprise me a bit if he did! He saw the gates of hell tremble and the foundations of Satan's city, Pandemonium, shake because he had a vision of Satan's overthrow in the lives of the human family.

Tremble if you must and worry if you can't avoid it but know this: If you would have it so, Jesus is laughing out loud on your behalf until the day when you will be able to do it for yourself! In him you're day is coming! Your triumph has been secured! You and the Lord Jesus Christ will sit down together and laugh till your sides split!

# 24

## THERE'S NO GOD—SO WHAT?

I have a single point to make! I don't wish to argue here that there is a God but I wish to say that anyone with a heart would surely wish there was a God worthy of worship and service; such a God that caring people would be happy to throw in with him "the stubborn ounces of their weight" in a glorious enterprise.

Robert Wright asked outspoken atheist, Daniel Dennett, if he was an atheist. DD said he didn't particularly care for the term's connotations but, yes, he was an atheist though he didn't make a deal of it, he said. [He has written three books advocating it and is very involved in a movement for atheists "coming out of the closet," so to speak. I would say that's "making a deal out of it" but if Christians and other theists have a right to spread their views why wouldn't atheists?] Wright asked him, "Do you wish you could believe in God?" and Dennett immediately shot back, "No!" He misses nothing, you see, by not believing in God and feels no need of him.

It isn't, he said, that he *passionately* denies there's a God, it's more like, he said, "*Of course there's no God,* but so what?"

Religious people can be incredibly self-centered and they rightly get a lot of stick for it, but atheists of the Dennett, Weinberg, Dawkins and Harris kind have no eye for others either. I don't know if Bob Geldof is an atheist but I do know that despite his social usefulness he's *glad* (he said) that death is nothing but an endless sleep. I don't know Dennett but his "so what?" makes it clear he hasn't thought with sufficient compassion about the teeming millions of innocents and defenseless who have gone down under the cruel hordes ancient and modern. I'm more disappointed in Bob Geldof who has seen the agony of the world right up close and has worked hard to do something about it. Having seen the cruelty and abuse that these peoples have been subjected to generation after generation I don't understand how Bob can be pleased with the story that life and all hope for justice and restitution ends at the grave. Nazis rape, rob, torture and butcher you and your end is the grave. The Nazi lives in extravagance and pleasure until old age and goes to a painless sleep.

That—*that* doesn't set our teeth on edge? Well, there's no God to right all wrongs but "so what?"

If you asked Dennett if he cared about justice for the oppressed nations and classes in human society he might be offended—doesn't everyone? He confessed he had done some things wrong but that he was pretty much a good man (and I don't doubt that) but how can a good man *not* wish there was someone who would one day bring justice to the forgotten poor of the world? I'm not saying, at this point, that there is such a one, but how can we say we don't *wish* that there was such a one?

How could we *not* wish that even now the world was a place of righteousness, where nations worked together in the grand enterprise of abolishing disease and want and righting wrongs? Recognising our limitations and not living in ceaseless anguish about what we cannot do, still we must surely wish that some leader would rise up in the Middle East or in Zimbabwe or in Sudan and other centres of profound abuse and loss—we must wish at times for a leader to rise up and turn the whole damnable stream of abuse around and bring peace and prosperity and dignity to these places.

And if we wish that could be true via human hands for a long time to come how can we say we wouldn't wish it to be true via God on a permanent basis? Is Dennett so set against the idea that God is, that he wouldn't wish for humanity *someone* to make it up to the plundered poor?

**If** the Christian faith is true that there is a God who came to us in and as Jesus of Nazareth, revealing what his will would be on earth if we were to do it and calling Christians to keep the truth that Jesus is Lord and is coming to right all wrongs before the hearts and minds of the world, would that not be better than having to admit there is no justice or restitution for teeming millions? **If** that is true and Christians in their lives are to live out the purpose of God that will be completed when Jesus returns, would we not *wish* that were true for the crushed billions? I don't say we should pretend we believe it's true; only that if we care for more than our own satisfaction would we not *wish* there was someone who would make it all right for them?

*But it's clear that death is more than "natural". Whatever else is true about it, when it came as the judgement of God—and it did at some point—it was more than "natural"—it now had the notion of "penalty" and it carried with it the testimony that the human relationship with God had been distorted in some way. In light of the biblical witness, death continues to bear witness to this very day of that distortion of humanity's relationship with God.*

# 25

## THE DEATH OF A CHILD

God made us mortal, that is, subject to biological death so in that sense death is "natural". My guess is that since God gave Adam and Eve full and free invitation to eat of every tree in the garden except the tree of knowledge of good and evil (Genesis 2:16-17) that they were eating of "the tree of life" and it counteracted their mortality. It makes no sense to me that they would eat of all the others trees in the garden except the one that sustained life; so I'm assuming they ate of it. Would you not eat of it if God freely offered it?

From the moment they were cut off from the tree the death process was on its way to the inevitable end God had appointed. Even if all we had to say about it was that it was "natural", it would still be true that death was ordained by God since that's how he made us—mortal, subject to death. Death in that sense is not unnatural because that was how God created us—mortal! He did not create us mortal because we had already sinned before he created us.

No, he created us susceptible to death and then we chose to sin against him.

But it's clear that death is more than "natural". Whatever else is true about it, when it came as the judgement of God—and it did at some point—it was more than "natural"—it now had the notion of "penalty" and it carried with it the testimony that the human relationship with God had been distorted in some way. In light of the biblical witness, death continues to bear witness to this very day of that distortion of humanity's relationship with God.

At the very beginning, death as penalty and judgement would only have meant something to Adam and Eve. That aspect of death would not have related to any of their infant children should they have died. God doesn't punish the innocent! Nevertheless, since Adam and Eve closed the door to all their descendants to the tree of life, whatever God thought of infants, they died because of something Adam and Eve did; they died because they were part of Adam's family and because God had made them mortal.

I'm presuming that this is what Paul had in mind when he said that in Adam all died (1 Corinthians 15:21-22). It wasn't that humans were inherently immortal before Adam sinned and as a consequence they became mortal; that's not true. As the Bible tells it, God cut off the mortal humans from the tree of life in response to Adam's rebellion. It didn't matter after that if a human could have been sinless—he was mortal and without something to counteract that mortality he died!

Setting aside for the moment questions generated by Romans 5:19 where Paul says by one man's disobedience all were made sinners, let me make the point again that God does not punish the innocent! We might do that and at times, God forgive us, we do that at times but God forbids it.

This means that when an infant dies it is no punishment from God! The infant certainly dies because it is not able to stay alive; it is mortal—subject to death. But in addition to that, like the rest of us the child was cut off from the source that offset human mortality. Unless we believe that an infant is actually and really guilty the idea that its death is punishment is intolerable! Since it's obvious that infants have committed no personal wrongs the only way to justify their being punished is to say that they truly did sin in Adam's sin. It won't do to say that God holds them guilty though he knows they're not really guilty. Simply saying he would do that sounds like a slander against the Holy Father! With the theological "realists" of the Reformed camp we'd be compelled to say that these infants actually sinned in Adam's sin (though Augustine and Calvin admitted they didn't know how that could be). They feel obliged to say that, don't you see, for it's "the soul that sins" that shall die for sin (see Ezekiel 18:20 and Deuteronomy 24:16). To credit to infants (or anyone else) what we know they didn't do would be heinous to us though we are great sinners; what would it be but the profoundest moral chaos for the Holy Father to hold them guilty of what he knows they aren't guilty of?

To get away with the claim that the death of an infant is punishment for its sin (committed in Adam) you have to do what Calvin and Augustine did—say it must be true because God wouldn't otherwise punish the child.

Nevertheless, it is true than in Adam even infants die! Why is that? Well, part of the answer I've suggested above—they were cut off from a source that counteracted human mortality; but there's more to it than that. These innocent infants are caught up in God's purpose to fulfil his creation commitment to the human family.

Amos 4:6-11 tells us of famines and droughts and pestilence that God sent to bring apostate Israel back home to him that he might forgive and bless them. The judgements were chastisement for sin committed; in this case the hardships wouldn't have existed if Israel had not gone off after other gods. Babies born during these droughts and famines suffered and they suffered under the judgements God poured out to redeem the apostates but the babies were the innocent suffering along with the guilty. Let me repeat: the drought the child suffered from existed because of sin and the child shared the hurt and death that the drought brought but God wasn't punishing the child. The child died but it wasn't the same death the impenitent apostate died. [What difference does it make if the child still dies? It makes all the difference in the world. The children of an imprisoned embezzler are left without a father but they aren't punished for what their father did.]

The infant in Amos' day died from a famine that God deliberately sent in response to Israelite sin. The existence of the judgement had nothing to do with the infants! It had all to do with sinning Israelites; it had all to do with the guilty! But the instrument of God's judgement (the famine and such) takes the lives of the innocent children (and the devoted servants of God in Israel) who die in the punishment of Israel.

God will not spare even the innocent (see Romans 8:32).

The death of all the children, the death of a single child is the damning evidence of our guilt and a witness to God's relentless pursuit of humanity to redeem it. We need not worry—such children are in good hands.

# 26

## PERSONAL FAITH AND CHRIST'S TRIUMPH

In 1 Timothy 3:16 Paul says, "Beyond all question, the mystery of godliness is great" and then proceeds to summarise the faith by quoting a well-established Christian confession that has a series of mind-boggling truths. The incarnation is a brain-wrecker, vindicated by the Spirit is too rich and complex and taken "up" in glory is a centre of controversy. Seen by angels is plain enough if it weren't so mysterious and preached on among the nations makes perfect sense (who would want to keep a message like that to herself?). But what do you make of that "believed on in the world"?

Believed on in heaven, believed on inside the jewelled walls and down the golden streets of the city foursquare, but believed on "in the world"? This world? The one you and I live in? The one you and I and millions with us have helped to build with lies and treachery and uncleanness and self-centeredness? Believed on in this world? Where Roman armies exiled enslaved millions and called it re-settlement, where they committed genocide and called it discipline, the one in which they created a desert and called it peace and where degenerate aristocrats fed their educated slaves to pet fishes? Did Paul mean this, our world? The one that educates its children from infancy how to be greedy while calling it "just good business", providing them with lots of good reasons to be racist, teaching them how to sneer at goodness and holiness while calling verbal or visual filth art?

Are we talking about this world, the one that hated and hounded him? The world of tough politicians that had no time for talk of crosses or integrity while there is more money and power to be gained? The world of churchgoing people that is good at singing and eating Passovers and Lord's Suppers and "doing church" and writing books about the love of God while harbouring bitterness, nurturing unbridled ambition, becoming experts at self-excusing, all neatly packaged in a sickening self-righteousness? My world?

Yes, it's astonishing, but even in a world like this one Jesus has been able to persuade people to believe in him!

Paul and people like him, down to this very day, have come to desperate people that have been oppressed externally and internally, socially and morally to the point where hope had died and cynicism was king; they came to people like that and gave them a Message and praise God, incredible though it seems, they believed!

Now that's a great mystery. I know that when Paul used "mystery" he meant something now revealed but you're dreaming if you think just because it's been revealed that it's no mystery to us. How does it come that Jesus Christ was believed on in a world like this?

The faith of any individual in Jesus Christ is astonishing. We take its existence too much for granted. We tend not to think much about it, of course, but when we do many of us take it as almost "natural" that we believe. "Well, of course, we believe, what's the surprise in that, isn't Christ worth believing in?" Yes, of course he is worth believing in but it isn't the worthiness of Christ that I'm amazed at. What astonishes me is that people shaped for so long by sin in a world that is really lord Sin's empire have stopped believing in Sin and now believe in Jesus Christ.

We stress the truth that there is no faith in Christ without a free commitment to him as if that explained the existence of our faith. Look, it's precisely because we were blessed with free will that we were able to become sinners in the first place. Free will doesn't explain the existence of faith in Christ. How does it come that we freely believed in him when the world was and is all-encompassing? How did we ever get free from it? Did we free ourselves by our moral strength? Did we face lord Sin, denounce and renounce him out of the moral and spiritual strength that we had without God's help? You understand I'm not talking about intellectual capacity at this moment, I'm talking about the amazing moral truth that at some point we turned to emperor Sin, defied him and walked away from him to Jesus Christ! That's called repentance. How did that come about?

It came about because God in the crucified Christ disarmed the powers and defeated lord Sin and came in the gospel and told us he had done it. Had he not done that there would be no faith in Jesus Christ on earth. And the faith of every believer and the corporate faith of the church make visible and concrete the triumph of Jesus Christ over Sin and the corrupted powers. The grand biblical truth shows itself in actual individuals and congregations. So the believers should rejoice in their personal deliverance from sin's dominion but, additionally, they should rejoice because they are witnesses to something vast, something cosmic and they're witnesses to the glory of the crucified, risen and reigning Lord Jesus Christ. Isn't that astonishing?

If we proclaim the gospel that Jesus is Lord and has conquered Sin and the principalities and powers and someone should ask us for proof of that we would of course turn to scriptures. But it would be perfectly legitimate to point out the fact that we ourselves have faith in Jesus Christ and that is part of the proof that the gospel is God's saving power because we ourselves have been saved by faith. Scattered all over the world, little handfuls of people with no political or social clout, many of them despised and some of them persecuted by their communities, families and even governments are living proof of Christ's Lordship because he overcame the sin in them and brought them to faith! Their personal faith and salvation is proof that God in Jesus Christ actually saves people (1 Corinthians 1:21 and Romans 1:16). Rome slew him and yet here he is saving people by bringing them to faith in him.

As long as the world stands there's a man who will be known as "the penitent thief" whose faith climbed over every conceivable obstacle to breathe free. Despite his background, his own agony, the appearance of the one dying across from him that said he was nothing more than a criminal like himself he said, "Lord, remember me when you come into your kingdom." That faith wasn't born in a soft home and comfortable circumstances and it was more than a personal commitment of faith. That personal faith was a proof that there, on that other cross, the world and all the principalities and powers were being stripped of their power and dignity (Colossians 2:15).

And some of you reading this know very well what crucifixion means but every day and in every way by God's grace your faith in Jesus Christ leads you to say, "Lord remember me when..."

And because of it, if you listen really hard, from some vast distance you'll be able to hear the threshing sound and the pain-filled screech of a fatally wounded Dragon who knows his time is short.

# 27

## BURNING BUSHES & GOING BAREFOOT

Sometimes you see or hear things and you just feel like taking your shoes off because something has made the entire place seem holy. Such things often are but they don't need to be overtly religious to fill you with awe (which is always religious in nature). Depending on your background and experience you only have to look at a starry sky or a waterfall or a field of wheat or a tiny baby or the devotion of one human to another and you're unzipped; life is never the same even though you go back to the "ordinary". You've seen something you can't unsee, heard something you can't unhear. A chicken might as well try to get back into the shell it broke out of as it would be for us to live as if we hadn't seen this wondrous thing.

It's true; sometimes the holy is there and we don't realise it until later. It's only when we become sensitive to such that we realise we've seen a burning bush and not just another somewhat interesting occurrence ["yes, that was…um…interesting," a big yawn and a stretch, "so what's on television this evening?"].

Each of us has his/her own moments [don't we?] though some public domain events can affect us all the same way.

It was only years after she died that I realised this was so about my mother (who bore thirteen of us and raised nine of us to adulthood). I was in the presence of a burning bush and didn't know it—I was too busy, too young, too something. I should have gone barefoot—I was on holy ground.

The trouble was, I had seen others like my mother (but not at all exactly like her) and I suppose I was used to the sight. Her life wasn't out-in-the-open different and gob-smacking as Dick Hoyt's wondrous devotion to his son Rick, that thankfully made headlines a while back; but my mother's was as real and genuine and lasting and, in some ways (the details don't matter), even more costly. Moses must have seen a lot of bushes burning in that wilderness heat but he'd never seen "a burning bush," if you know what I mean. There's was nothing ordinary about this sight on that day and there was nothing ordinary about the presence of God in my mother. Some of you know exactly what I mean for you have seen "a burning bush" and the feeling that you should go barefoot is appropriate.

# *28*

## NATURAL CALAMITIES & ETERNAL TORMENT

When people (like me) say that God is ultimately responsible for calamities today a host runs to defend him against what they see to be *an accusation!* Why do they run to say, "God didn't do that"? Because of the destruction and loss of property, financial security, peace of mind and loss of loved ones.

Yes, it's true that that's what calamities bring—they're worse than we can grasp and certainly worse than we can say, but why do people run to defend God against the claim that God brought this about?

*They do it because they think that if God did such a thing he would have done something indefensible.* You hear them say this over and over again—"God wouldn't do a think like that!"

That same host that says God wouldn't do such a thing don't mind preaching that one of these days God will begin to eternally consciously torture people in a lake of fire (or some form of eternal conscious torture).

*And who is it that is going to do this?* The God they say can't be responsible for bringing about a calamity in our days!

Many in that same host insist that one of these days God is going to set fire to this whole earth and burn it until its very basic elements melt (they use 2 Peter 3 to make their point).

Their favourite preachers are fond of grinning and shouting in their sermons that all the businesses and buildings and houses and possessions on the entire earth are going to burn "in the Big Fire". And who do they say is going to burn the earth to cinders and destroy all the businesses that people have spent years building? The same God that they say wouldn't bring a calamity like Katrina or the Asian tsunami. He's willing to ceaselessly torture multiplied millions forever but it would be unworthy of him to bring calamity here and now? Make sense of that for me!

## No wonder some thoughtful non-believers look at us and shake their heads in unbelief.

Then after telling us that God is in no way responsible for such happenings they defend us for getting mad at God when such events happen!

You've heard their leaders preach that—haven't you? "Get mad at God. He understands and he doesn't want you to act like grovelling dogs. You remember how he listened to Job raving and raging and still thought him to be righteous. Tell God you're mad at him. He won't destroy you for it."

But mad at him for what? They tell us he had nothing to do with any of our awful pain or loss and then they encourage us to be mad at him so that our faith will be "authentic"! Get mad at God for what?

One leading religious light on a TV show some time back insisted that Katrina wasn't the will of God and he concluded his remarks about the matter saying that people should, "Play it down and pray it up."

Good grief!

# 29

## THIS I BELIEVE

I believe that God lived in eternal, joy-filled and holy fellowship in what C.S Lewis called "the land of the Trinity". The Father and Son enjoyed fellowship one with another through the Holy Spirit and rising out of that triune fellowship came the purpose to create, that the life and joy of God would be experienced beyond the Godhead.

I believe that Jesus is and was fully and completely and without addition or subtraction a man. But he was and is God being a man. Not a man being a man or an angel being a man or an exalted creature being a man—Jesus is nothing less and nothing other than God being a man.

I believe that as the creation purpose was conceived that "Jesus" was not only the agent by which creation came into being, he was the guiding thought and inspiration that shaped and determined the final form that creation would take. In addition to that, "Jesus" was the one for whom the creation came into being, that is, not only would he be the supreme expression of creation completed he would be the one glorified above all by the creation. This is Colossians 1:15-16.

I believe until the now immortal Lord of all, Jesus Christ, completes this phase of his royal reign by obliterating death for all others as he has conquered it himself that God's creative purpose will not be completed. Genesis 1 was only the beginning of the creation of God that ultimately had Jesus in view.

I believe that with humanity's fall in Adam and Eve the entire creation was dragged under the curse (compare Colossians 1:16 and 2:15) and that God's creative purpose could not be accomplished without the death of Jesus. Paul said (Colossians 1:19-20) that God "reconciled all things in heaven and on earth" to himself through the blood of Christ.

I believe that the life and cross of Christ cannot be separated from the resurrection, glorification and exaltation of Jesus Christ for it is in and through them that the new creation has begun in the person of Jesus Christ. Nevertheless, while these are inextricably and essentially linked they are conceptually distinct—the cross is pivotal though never to be isolated.

I believe that in dying (and rising) Jesus accomplished something that is independent of creation's response. It is something already accomplished, fully and without reservation--he has become and is Lord of all! The sovereignty over the entire creation has come into the hands of a human--one human, Jesus Christ, the last Adam and the second man (1 Corinthians 15:45, 47). Nothing has been the same since the death--exaltation of Jesus. By his death has Jesus actually accomplished anything? Yes, he has become Lord over all and because he is the Lord over all that has cosmic consequences. Let me repeat: this has been actually accomplished whether or not humanity confesses it or cares about.

I believe the creation Jesus inherited was not like the creation the first Adam inherited. The creation under the first Adam came to him as "very good" and under his dominion it came to ruin. The creation that came to the last Adam had been estranged from God and he brought it all under his own sovereignty and reconciled it to his Holy Father (Colossians 1:19-20, Ephesians 1:10, 1 Peter 3:22).

I believe that what makes the creation "new" is that Jesus, the second man, is steering and bringing it to what God purposed it to be when he first created it in light of his plan before the world was. What makes it a new creation is the purpose and spirit of Jesus who is Lord of all—he means to glorify his Holy Father in the exercise of his dominion as surely as the first Adam dishonoured the Father.

I believe that God's massive enterprise is for the entire human race—without exception. The life and death and exaltation of Jesus Christ was purposed to benefit the entire creation. See Romans 8:18-39.

I believe that to gain his purpose God elected people at various times and places to be his chosen. They were chosen—Israel illustrates—to enjoy life with God in a peculiar relationship that they might bear witness to his creation purpose—a purpose he never lost sight of though humanity sinned. The elect were chosen unto salvation and mission (2 Thessalonians 2:13-14 and Ephesians 3:10, 21). Their mission is to be a standing witness that God has reconciled the entire creation to himself in Jesus Christ.

I believe that the cosmic reconciliation of "all things" is experienced in various ways depending on the nature of the specific "things" embraced in the "all things". Sinners, for example, are reconciled to God by his not reckoning their sins against them (2 Corinthians 5:19). I believe that the purpose of God is not exhausted in the salvation of the elect but that he offers the fruit of the redeeming, restoring and regenerating work of Jesus Christ to the non-elect (see 1 John 2:2, 1 Timothy 4:10, 2 Peter 2:1).

I believe that to take all the texts that speak of the elect and their place and role in God's unfolding of his creation purposes and conclude that that is the complete story is a serious misunderstanding of God's relationship and commitment to humanity. As surely as elect Israel did not exhaust the saving and blessing work of God in pre-Christ ages neither does his NT elect exhaust his saving and blessing work in this the Christian era.

I believe that election is the work of God through his Spirit who brings people to faith in Jesus Christ by the gospel (Philippians 1:29, Romans 10:13-15, 2 Thessalonians 2:13-14, 1 Corinthians 1:21) and brings them into covenant relationship with God (Ephesians 2:11-22, 2 Corinthians 3:3-6).

I believe that the non-elect who have not heard the call of God by the gospel are not a single group. Along with the millions who care nothing for God or the higher life there are those who look for higher life (though they have not heard the gospel of Jesus Christ) and that they by patient continuance in well doing will gain glory, honour and immortality through the work of Jesus (Romans 2:6-16 and compare Acts 17:24-27).

I believe that those who hear the gospel of our Lord Jesus Christ and refuse it suffer eternal loss.

# 30

## THE TREES WILL CLAP THEIR HANDS

I was bathing Ethel and singing Isaiah 55:12 where he said the mountains will break into singing and the trees of the field with clap their hands. I asked her, "Why do you think the trees will clap their hands?" She said, "Probably because they're happy!" With that she was done. Her quick response was right on target but I was looking for more and she wasn't in the position to breathe and discuss theology at the same time.

The biblical witness tells us that at the great Rebellion, when the human race began its runaway madness and thought they'd do better with their self-created destiny—the biblical witness tells us that the earth was cursed (Genesis 3:17). It wasn't Man that cursed it, though it was the humans that triggered the curse. God cursed it (Genesis 5:29) and he cursed it, he said, "because of you" (Genesis 3:17)!

As the Bible tells it, the non-human creation's "well-being" and destiny is linked inextricably with the human's relationship with God. Obviously the creation is not a choosing or self-conscious entity but the human dependence on creation is witnessed by the fact that it was out of the earth that God created the humans and it is out of the earth that God gives humans their sustenance. We can say what we like about wealth and political clout but you can't eat or drink those things even though the power structures can keep food and drink from the powerless and poor. In the end, what we need to keep us alive at the simple biological level comes from the earth.

By the will of God the creation protests against the human perversion of power. The nature of that protest is that the creation withholds from the human family that which God initially had purposed for it to give. God gave the humans dominion over creation (Genesis 1:26-28) to live with it in his image. The face of God that we see in creation is the face of a life-bringer, a harmony and peace-bringer; we see someone who enables all to flourish and grow in the place he gave them. Creation's lord (humankind) fell through sin from its place of glory and the creation that was a witness to and an expression of that glory was brought down with mankind. The human family that tumbled down toward futility was matched by a creation that as a consequence reflected the human fall. As the humans withheld from their Lord what was due him so the creation withheld from its lord what was due him. The peace and harmony that was experienced within the created sphere was pretty well shattered.

Paul says in Romans 8:19-22 that the creation groans in its frustration or futility and eagerly looks forward to the time when the children of God are manifested in glory because then it will be liberated from its present futility and frustration. Under its shameful lord it cannot be all that it was created to be but the Lord God made it and tied its fortunes to the human lord. Nevertheless, in withholding from its human lord the glory initially given to him the creation is bearing witness to the judgement of God against that human lord. The creation, whatever its frustration at being implicated in the Fall takes God's side in the resultant situation.

After we've admitted some issues we can't settle about the Genesis 3:17-19 and get to its central thrust, what's the text saying to us and what does it mean by what it says to us? Whatever else it says it tells us this. By the will and wisdom of God the creation cannot finally be at peace with the human family as long as the human family is not finally at peace with God. This close tie between the creation and the humans is reflected throughout the entire biblical record.

Leviticus 18:24-28 has God saying this to Israel, "Do not defile yourself in any of these ways, because this is how the nations that I am going to drive out before you became defiled. Even the land was defiled; so I punished it for its sins, and the land vomited out its inhabitants...And if you defile the land, it will vomit you out as it vomited out the nations that were before you."

Yes, I can see there are numerous things to be worked out. But after we've made room for "anthropomorphism" and the like, what does the text tell us about the land and what does it mean by what it tells us about the land? It tells us at least this: land as pictured in such a text is opposed to human wickedness and it acts as God's instrument in punishing the wickedness.

But we're to notice how close the relationship is between land and people. The land out of which humans are created and which sustains them is "punished [paqad] for its sins." What that means, precisely, isn't spelled out but other texts come to our aid. Just the same, though it is "punished for its sins" the land is related to God in his aversion to human sin and vomits the sinners out. [The entire notion of "visiting" iniquity needs to be looked at with care.]

God "visits" the sins committed in the land on the land itself. The land experiences drought and famine and pestilence and desolation. It is left unattended and becomes wild, people avoid it think it is jinxed; they call it a "devourer of its people."

Here's how Ezekiel 36:1-15 has it. God tells Ezekiel to address the land of Israel. He is not to talk about the land but to speak to the land. "Son of man, prophesy to the mountains of Israel and say, 'O mountains of Israel, hear the word of the Lord...Because they ravaged and hounded you from every side so that you became the possession of the rest of the nations and the object of people's malicious talk and slander...This is what the Sovereign Lord says...because you have suffered the scorn of the nations...I swear with uplifted hand that the nations around you will suffer scorn. But you, O mountains of Israel, will produce branches and fruit...I am concerned for you and will look on you with favor; you will be plowed and sown, and I will multiply the number of people on you...I will increase the number of men and animals upon you...I will settle people on you as in the past. I will cause people, my people Israel, to walk upon you. They will posses you, and you will be their inheritance; you will never again deprive them of their children. Because people say to you, 'You devour men and deprive your nation of its children,' therefore you will no longer devour or make your nation childless."

You'd think God was speaking to a person when you read this sort of thing. It looks like the land consciously chose to throw its people out. But 36:16-21 makes it clear that it's God that makes exiles of his sinning people. But what extraordinary speech it is that ties the land so closely to the sins of the people and the judgement against them.

And what astonishing speech it is that teaches us that when the people of God are manifested in completed glory with their Lord that the eager creation will share in the liberation of God's people and become the place where righteousness dwells. See Romans 8:16-23.

# *31*

## WILL THE CREATION ABIDE FOREVER?

I don't believe God has purposed to utterly obliterate this creation. I believe in light of Genesis 317-19, 5:29 in particular and Genesis 3—8 in general (and see Romans 8:19-20) that God cursed the creation and that in Jesus Christ that curse is removed (see Romans 8:20-23). In the hymn Jesus Saves we sing "Earth shall keep her Jubilee, Jesus saves, Jesus saves."

The year of Jubilee, of course, was the year of a new beginning (see Leviticus 25:8-17, 50-55). After seven cycles of seven years (sabbatical years) the Year of Jubilee was the fiftieth. The blowing of the ram's horn (shophar) on the Great Day of Atonement signalled national cleansing and a new start that embraced the entire nation. Jubilee was the eighth year after seven sevens; it was eight, the number of new beginnings. Toil on the land was forbidden that year and the land freely gave the nation its food. All debts were cancelled and prisoners were freed (details were worked out) and the land inheritance returned to the original owners, those to whom God gave it (as stewards—for the land always remained God's land and could not be sold in perpetuity).

I believe that the final removal of the curse is heralded in the Year of Jubilee and shadowed in passages like Ezekiel 47:1-12 and Revelation 21:1—22:22 with their "return to Eden" speech. Ezekiel and Revelation have their own specific agendas but as surely as every judgement shadows the Final Judgement every blessing and triumph for God's people heralds the Final Triumph. (See how the song of Mary begins with God's grace to her but is then taken as the assurance of grace to all—Luke 1:46-55. The psalms are saturated with that kind of "he did it for me therefore he will do it for all" kind of praise.)

But aren't there texts, which plainly say that the creation will be destroyed? Well, there are a few (not nearly as many as people suppose) that look like that. The core text, I suppose, is in 2 Peter 3:1-13. I'm purposing to say something about it in another place.

Luke 21:33 (see also Matthew 24:35 and Mark 13:31) seems to predict that the creation will be destroyed. "Heaven and earth will pass away, but my words will never pass away," Jesus Christ said. Matthew 5:18 offers something similar. "Until heaven and earth disappear, not the smallest letter, not the least stroke of a pen, will by any means disappear from the Law until everything is accomplished."

I don't think these texts are affirming the destruction of creation. I think Jesus is affirming the changeless certainty of his word and I think he does it by saying what he did. I think he is saying (in essence), "You'll see the heavens and earth pass away before you see my word fail." In the Matthew 5:18 text he is not speaking of his own word but of the Jewish Law. I don't think it matters, however, because his point is the same.

I think what is happening in these texts is that Jesus Christ is taking what humans regard as permanent and certain to be around, come what may, and he is using it to illustrate the abiding nature of his own word (or God's). "You look at the unchanging creation and make that a standard of what abides. I tell you my word is even more sure."

Let me illustrate further what I mean. Ecclesiastes 1:4 says this. "Generations come and generations go, but the earth remains forever." That closing phrase denies that the earth will pass away.

In Psalm 78:69 a singer praises God for his faithfulness to a faithless people. He's especially pleased that God chose David's house and built Zion. Here's what he said of Jerusalem, "He built his sanctuary like the heights, like the earth that he established forever." No matter how faithless Israel is, Jerusalem is secure and because God dwells there it's like the very mountains on which it sits and it will abide like the earth God established forever.

Now I don't believe that either of those texts is affirming anything about how long the creation will abide. They have a different agenda and point to make. They want to say something about how faithful God is (in the psalm) and how fleeting and vain human life is (as in Ecclesiastes). To do it they make use of the abiding nature of creation. Habakkuk 3:6 speaks of "ancient mountains [and] age-old hills"—unmoved until God moved them. Be sure to read that text though none of them are discussing how long the creation will be around. That's not their point.

One more illustration from Jeremiah. Judah is about to go into captivity and that will complete the exile of the entire nation. Many were thinking and some were saying that God no longer cared for Israel and that his faithfulness had come to an end but Jeremiah 30—33 sets that nonsense right. God assures them that his promises would never fail and his covenants with Israel would be honoured. And how does he do that?

Jesus said, "My faithfulness will last longer than heaven and earth." God says, "My faithfulness will last as long as heaven and earth."

Jesus Christ said, "You will see the creation obliterated before you will see my word come to nothing." God says the opposite! He says, "You can be as sure of my word as you can be that the sun and moon will always be in the heavens!"

Here's what he says in Jeremiah 31:35-36. "This is what the Lord says, he who appoints the sun to shine by day, who decrees the moon and stars to shine by night...only if these decrees vanish from my sight, declares the Lord, will the descendants of Israel ever cease to be a nation before me."

Again in Jeremiah 33:19-26 he says this. "This is what the Lord says: If you can break my covenant with the day and my covenant with the night, so that day and night no longer come at their appointed time, then my covenant with David my servant—and my covenant with the Levites who are priests ministering before me—can be broken...Have you not noticed that these people are saying, 'The Lord has rejected the two kingdoms he chose'? So they despise my people and no longer regard them as a nation. This is what the Lord says: If I have not established my covenant with day and night and the fixed laws of heaven and earth, then I will reject the descendants of Jacob and David my servant and will not choose one of his sons to rule over the descendants of Abraham, Isaac and Jacob. For I will restore their fortunes and have compassion on them."

In these texts God says they could be as sure of his word to Israel as they could of his covenant with creation. Some were saying God had rejected Israel and broken the covenants he made with them because he wanted nothing more to do with them. He tells them that that would only happen when there was no more sun or moon or stars. He says his covenants with Israel were as permanent and as sure as the fixed laws of nature. He assures them that as long as the sun, moon and stars are in their places he would be faithful to his covenants with Israel.

But while it's reasonable enough to infer that such texts teach the creation will never cease, that is not their point. The creation is called in as something that is around when all the humans pass away and when God wants to illustrate how sure his promises are he says, "They're as sure as the creation! My promises will last as long as the creation!" It's a comparison thing. For obvious reasons he wouldn't say, "My promises are as sure as a flower of the field." Jesus Christ used a flower of the field as an illustration of something passing and he used heaven and earth as an illustration of something permanent. Jesus would not have said, "A flower of the field will die before my word will come to nothing." People see flowers dying every day but they don't see mountain ranges vanishing and creations passing away.

We've seen that God likens his enduring faithfulness to the enduring reliability of the creation (under his covenant, of course)—

his faithfulness last as long as the creation lasts. But look what a psalmist does in Psalm 102:25-26. He contrasts God's abiding nature with the passing nature of the creation.

"In the beginning you laid the foundation of the earth, and the heavens are the work of your hands. They will perish, but you remain; they will all wear out like a garment. Like clothing you will change them and they will be discarded. But you remain the same, and your years will never end."

So what does all that mean?

It means we should look carefully at what a writer or speaker means to do with what he says even if he/they speak on the same subject. Jeremiah says the creation never ends and so it illustrates God's faithfulness, which never ends. Jesus Christ says, in comparison with the abiding nature of my words the creation is a passing affair.

*Colossians 1:15-17 makes us think of Genesis 1:26-28. The echo of the "image of God" and then the notion of dominion and power in which Jesus is said to be pre-eminent and the one in whom all things hold together. Colossians 1 echoes Genesis 1 but it takes us light years beyond it.*

# 32

## THE CREATION IS "FOR" JESUS

John and others have taught us that God must be understood through Jesus Christ—if you've seen and known me you see and know the Father, Jesus taught us (John 14); and if we've come to know Jesus we've come to know the Holy Spirit who is the Spirit of God's Son as well as the Spirit of God (Galatians 4:6).

When we think of knowing God by looking at Jesus I would suppose that we automatically think of God's *character* and the kind of heart he has; no bad thing that. But I think we need we should spare a thought for God's *purposes.* His purposes reflect his character too, don't you know, but Jesus came to accomplish things in his Father's name and as his Father's servant and when we see Jesus we see the one in whom the purposes of God are focused.

Colossians 1:15-17 makes us think of Genesis 1:26-28. The echo of the "image of God" and then the notion of dominion and power in which Jesus is said to be pre-eminent and the one in whom all things hold together. Colossians 1 echoes Genesis 1 but it takes us light years beyond it. Three distinct prepositions tell us how and why the creation came to be. It came to be "through" him as the agent of creation (1 Corinthians 8:6). As surely as election and redemption is "in" Jesus so also was the world created "in" him (see Ephesians 1:4). He is the conceptual sphere within which God worked to create; creation was created in light of Jesus, with Jesus as its driving thought and inspiration. And the creation was created for (or "unto") him—he was creation's goal. In the glorious and immortal Jesus, the Son of God and the last Adam the creation found its completion. What went before was real and wonderful but it was all moving toward him. This God purposed in creation before the human family rebelled and our rebellion did not change his mind. The redeeming life and person of Jesus Christ completes the two tasks—he sets the world right in redemption and brings it to its purposed climax with him as its glorified Lord.

The Incarnation, redeeming life, death, resurrection and exaltation confirm God's eternal creation purposes by bringing about redemption and reconciliation. The creation is not destined for destruction in "the great fire"—it was created *for* Jesus.

This has ramifications for how we look at, work with and relate to the creation.

# 33

## WHAT'S CHRISTIAN ABOUT CHRISTIAN FAITH?

The "obedience of faith" is shorthand for "the obedience of faith in Jesus Christ." It is the phrase "in Jesus Christ" that makes the Christian's faith distinctive and distinguishes it from all other faith.

The obedience of faith in Jesus Christ is not simply obedience to a moral standard. Others before us have been obedient to moral law (some more and some less) but for obvious reasons their obedience was not the "obedience of faith in Jesus Christ."

The "obedience of faith" for an Old Testament saint (see Hebrews 11, for examples) is the obedience that would rise out of his or her trust in God as he had revealed himself. It would be as genuine and as real as the Christian obedience of faith in Jesus Christ. But obedience of faith in Jesus Christ is distinctive; it is shaped by and expresses the developed purpose of God that has come to its completion only in Jesus Christ (compare Hebrews 11:39-40 as illustrative of what I mean). The OT obedience of faith could not have the content of the NT obedience of faith precisely because the Christ had not been revealed and the purpose of God had not come to completion in the person and work of Jesus Christ.

The obedience of faith in Jesus Christ is never less than but it is always more than an individual submitting him or herself to Christ. It's more than saying, "I trust you and will do what is right." The Christ's faith is Christ-shaped! It is more than doing good because Christ was good. The Christian's faith is acceptance of and commitment to Christ's person and agenda and method. It is the Christian's faith that constitutes him or her a Christian.

It's important to understand that the obedience of faith in the OT or the NT was not just about an individual's inner world. Biblical faith is never simply a personal response! Israel's faith—a faith common to all the individuals that made up the nation—wasn't just about their moral response by individuals that wanted to be "saved". The faith expressed in Israel's ordinances, liturgy, festivals, behaviour and so forth was a witness to the nature, character and deeds of God as he had revealed himself. Israel's united response of faith proclaimed things like God's faithfulness to Abrahamic promises and his rescue from Egypt and the wilderness and his bringing them into the land he promised. If we had watched Israel's life for a while we would have learned about their history and destiny under Yahweh and not just that they were nice honest mass of individuals who treated one another well. And we would have learned it because the national faith was designed to make it known! Their faith—as a nation and as individuals who were part of that nation—proclaimed an ongoing drama that God was unfolding and of which Israel was a part. In short, faith in the OT or NT was "gospeling" and not just the correct moral response to God.

But the NT "obedience of faith" bears witness to a part of the Story that wasn't yet available to Israel of pre-Christian times. The faith, ordinances and liturgy and lives of Christians as a corporate whole bear witness to the coming of God in and as Jesus Christ, of his life, death, burial, resurrection, exaltation and returning again and what those realities mean.

That is what's "Christian" about the Christian faith. To isolate our love for our families, our honesty in business or our patience under stress from the meaning of our faith and compare them with the same realities in non-Christians is a blunder. Our obedience that rises out of faith in Jesus Christ is so shaped and is to be immediately and inextricably connected with our role as the elect of God! Our lives of faith are designed to show that we have been called out of darkness into God's light to bear witness to Jesus Christ.

We are not simply "good living" people (though we ought to be pursuing a life og goodness). We are witnesses for God and what he has done! Isaiah 43:8-12 puts it in the plainest of terms. Israel has been evil in departing from God and he sent them into captivity; but now he brings them back home and the nations are called to see it all. Was Israel freed because the Medo-Persians liberated them or was it because God set them free? The nations are called to line up their witnesses to make their case and then God says to Israel "you are my witnesses." God had foretold all this and brought it to pass and Israel was the living proof of it. So it is with the Christian faith—it bears witness to God's ancient promises and their fulfilment in Jesus Christ.

It isn't all about you or me and about you and me "getting saved". It's bigger than that (though not less). It's about God and his eternal purpose and commitment toward the human family and how it is to be completed in Jesus Christ. That's what's Christian about the Christian faith.

*within the parameters of a gloriously "ordinary" life there is a way of seeing life, a way of fleshing out the gospel of Jesus Christ; there's a spirit that defies the world spirit that says we're to be all belly and pelvis and no head or heart.*

# 34

## SETTLING FOR LESS

Paul was a strange character. He careered off across half the world preaching ceaselessly about peace and freedom and seemed to have neither. Was there ever a man more driven? Was there ever a man who made himself a servant to so many? The truth is we know or know about thousands of men, women, boys and girls who were driven and joyfully discontent. They saw things and were seized by them and for love of them their whole lives were brought to heel in a holy obedience. The magic about such people is that their peace and freedom so out-strips our own that we don't recognise it as freedom and peace.

But in our more lucid moments we remember that true lovers find full freedom in their refusal to be free and that the most contented people are those who sell everything they have for a pearl of great price. Edmund Gosse got it right when he told about a swan that grew tired of the murky water and the narrow boundaries of the local pond, tired of the crumbs thrown to it and tired of the clinging reeds and the cramped space. (I've watched such swans in Ward Park, in a little pond not too far from where I live.) It headed out for distant places where the waters were cold, where the wind was often a gale and where many of its free bothers and sisters already were. And having done that, Gosse says, it never regretted what it tossed away. It refused to settle for less. And so it is, he thought, with all those glad, mad people who are a vision to behold and about whom we write songs and poetry.

*So sails the soul, and cannot rest,*
*Inglorious in the marsh of peace;*
*But leaves the good, to seek the best,*
*Though all its calms and comforts cease,—*
*Though what it seem'd to hold be lost,*
*Though that grow far which once was nigh—*
*By torturing hope in anguish tossed,*
*The awakened soul must sail or die.*

It just isn't possible for all of us to be Pauls; we have neither the temperament nor the specific calling for it; but it's certainly possible by God's grace to have the mind of Jesus Christ (Philippians 2:5) that so shapes our hearts and minds that we can't be satisfied with cheaper and lesser views of life and what it's all about.

Having found and been found by Jesus Christ Paul took a new view of all the good and wonderful things in his life—they took on a new complexion. Though they remained fine things that others might well enjoy he now saw them as so much rubbish (Philippians 3:4-8). But that is only a relative or comparative remark and he says it only because he compares those things with Jesus Christ. And as Jesus looked at his own status of equality with God and didn't see it as something to be exploited (2:5-7, NRSV) and so emptied himself Paul saw his giftedness and privilege in the same way. He gladly suffered the loss of those things because he wanted to be conformed to the image of Jesus Christ (Philippians 3:4-14).

Let me say it again: it isn't possible for each one of us to live out his or her life as Paul lived his out but within the parameters of a gloriously "ordinary" life there is a way of seeing life, a way of fleshing out the gospel of Jesus Christ; there's a spirit that defies the world spirit that says we're to be all belly and pelvis and no head or heart. Life can be lived in the spirit of Jesus in truth and vision and adventure—and it should be. Anything other and anything less is settling for less.

## 35

### ANGELS WITH DIRTY FACES

I only have to read scripture to know that people are walking contradictions and that some of us are breathing civil wars. Beyond that I simply have to look within to know that while what the Bible says seems very plain, what I see and feel within is absolutely beyond debate. And my experience with people confirms these two sources.

I don't say that we are all equally conflicted. I believe I know people that across the board are much more mature than I am. Yes, I suspect that on the whole they are more finely balanced and permeated to a greater degree with virtue than I am or ever have been. I would suppose if I were judged by my moral failures and weakness in some specific areas of my life that I would come very close to the bottom of the moral ladder. This is a great sadness to me for there is a part of me that longs for moral grandeur, there's a deep desire in me to be like the God in whose image I have been and am being created. [I mustn't give you the impression that people should be assessed on the basis of so many virtues over against so many vices—that would be wrong-headed, but I think you know what I mean by the above.]

I wish to make the point that however difficult it is for us to believe it, people are not just one thing. That should be—should it not?—a matter beyond dispute. Only the Christ was "just one thing".

I've known many people up close and personal who were faced with a choice between right and wrong and chose the wrong. But it has occurred to me that in many of those cases I was blessed in not being faced with the situation they were faced with; blessed with not having to make the choice between good and evil for I'm not at all certain that I would have stood where they fell.

Some poor souls are daily faced with the pressure to do evil while others of us (God be praised and thanked!) live in our morally cosy little routines. Surrounded by godly friends, provided with more than adequate material and social resources and having been shaped by strong and warm people and structures we are sheltered from many of the storms that beat ceaselessly around the heads of millions. Yes, surely there is profound reason to be grateful for our conditions but do they not underscore the moral disadvantage of the masses?

Is it surprising that so many are morally weak and fragmented? Given the social and cultural structures that promote the worst aspects of hedonism and greed and self-centredness, should we be surprised that masses fear neither God nor man? And if this is what they fight against from the moment they draw breath do we do well to feel nothing but revulsion and a desire to isolate or exterminate?

In a powerful television drama one of the characters is morally and mentally ill. He has killed repeatedly but due to the limits in the human judicial system he was not convicted. He attached himself to a lawyer, who, understandably, was afraid of him and wanted nothing to do with him. But the man felt the influence of this lawyer changing him for the better. He gets a job and purposes to live in goodness, free from the evils he had engaged in but the lawyer—again perfectly understandably—feels compelled to undermine his agenda. He's devastated by what he feels is betrayal and comes to say to her, "As you know, I have never denied being evil. One of the reasons I came to you initially—I saw you as my guardian out of evil and you in fact became that. I was beginning to turn my life around. I rediscovered hope and goodness and I credit much of that to your influence. But you walked away from me like I was some crazy, which I am at many levels. But my feelings for you...my friendship for you was sane and real and legitimate and good. It represents the part of me that wasn't ill or evil—it was good."

This expresses well what I want to say. I don't say that there can't be exceptions. I don't say that there are not people, who like Mephistopheles says in that other classic drama, "Evil be thou my good/ good be thou my evil." But I do say that such exceptions aside that there is not one of us that is "one thing". I do say that down somewhere in the mysterious depths of a human heart, along with its evil there can be the vestiges of good longed for, the residue of good purposes that died for lack of inner strength and outside help.

In the old movie Angels with Dirty Faces we have the hard-bitten and brutal gangster (played by Jimmy Cagney) going to the electric chair for multiple murders. He's arrogant, unrepentant and unafraid. For the sake of some boys who worship him as their hero the priest begs him to pretend he's afraid to die. Cagney goes to the chair kicking and screaming and begging for mercy—for the sake of the kids and because his friend asked him to do it.

Should we dismiss this as bleeding-heart drivel, nauseatingly sentimental and false to life? I think not. Hanging on a tree the young Lord of creation saw his enemies with their glittering eyes and heard their hoarse mocking and said, "Father, forgive them, they don't know what they're doing." Maybe it takes a purer and stronger heart than most of us have to speak this way under such circumstances. There's little doubt in my mind that the bulk of us when faced with someone we judge to be a threat have no wish to dwell on his or her virtues. The only thing that counts is their vice.

But when we gather in an assembly we're not slow to sing Rescue the Perishing. One of the stanzas has this neglected truth. "Down in the human heart/Crushed by the Tempter/Feelings like buried that grace can restore/Touched by a loving hand/Wakened by kindness/Chords that were broken will vibrate once more." This sounds well in four-part harmony and feels good during times of peace and tranquillity. But let me assume that for the most of us (certainly in the West) that actually doing something costly about such a truth is a real stretch, especially as the expression of our living out that truth on a daily basis. Maybe executing such conviction is beyond us—though it's possible for some that we know or have heard of. But I would suppose that before we can bear unbearable sorrow and fight unbeatable foes we need to truly think the unthinkable.

Ah well, then, so no one should be held accountable for wrongs done? I don't believe that. Even the Christ held accountable those he loved and pitied. But maybe we can quit pretending that we hold that all sin should be punished. We don't think all ours should be punished. Maybe we can chastise with less relish and more sensitivity. Maybe we can pity as well as punish. Maybe we can temper our speech when condemning the sins of others and perhaps we can renounce (if only to ourselves) the sense of moral superiority we feel. Should we ever judge? Of course we should! But surely not from a position of power, as though butter wouldn't melt in our own mouths. And should we ignore great evil because there is in the transgressor something of real worth? Oh, I'm certain we should not. I'm also certain of this, we should not ignore the something of real worth in him or her because there is great evil. And I'm certain we should take full measure of our own evil that lurks down among our virtues.

Wasn't it Albert Schweitzer who told us that two boys were wrestling in a school playground? It was a long and hard tussle but finally the bigger boy (Schweitzer) triumphed. The skinnier kid, panting, said something like. "You wouldn't have beaten me if I had been getting soup twice a day like you."

Hmmm, I wonder...

# 36

## A WAR FOR HEROES

When we're tired, bone tired and wishing there was some medicine we could take that would let us sleep for a thousand years, or at least until the war was over, we're tempted to doubt Paul's word. He says in 1 Corinthians 10:13, "No temptation has seized you except what is common to man." But that's just it, when we're weary we either don't believe that or we don't care if it's true. Mostly we tend to doubt it—our temptation is that bit different. At least we tend to think that about the mass of people though we know there are some whose furnace is ten times hotter than ours. (But they live in Third World countries, don't they?)

But Paul was sure that the temptations we experience have been experienced by others before us and are being experienced at this very moment. Nothing has happened to us, he goes on to say, that must take us away from God for God wouldn't permit a temptation about which we could do nothing. But his first remark is that our temptations are the common experience of our comrades. Everywhere he looked as he travelled through the world he saw earnest brothers and sisters putting on their armour to engage in war. War with an enemy that gives no quarter though it takes many as slaves! And it's the sight of these cheerfully serious people that lifts our spirits for the battle. "Here," she says, as we fumble with nervous finger to buckle something on, "let me help you." Alone with the noise of battle around us, alone and cut off from the main body we would have a hard time of it but shoulder to shoulder with people whose strength and heroism is disguised by their ordinary appearance we're made braver.

Nevertheless this is war! Real war; war against an enemy that seeks us out, meaning to end us and not just to harm us. Meaning not just to end us but to end all those we love and could learn to love. Take away the reality of this war and we face temptation unprepared, for the Lord Jesus has taught us that evil is a world spirit that would sift us as wheat and destroy us. We must allow no one to make us tremble in slavish fear as if the victory is not with us in the Christ. Still, we're not to think that sin and the fear it generates should be shrugged at as if it were not a killing power. In his Pilgrim's Progress John Bunyan helps us here when he tells us how Christian met Apollyon, the destroyer on the road to the Heavenly City.

Apollyon claims Christian as his unfaithful servant and Christian agrees that that is the case. He said he would serve Apollyon no more for he had given his life over to a young Prince whose government, company, country and service was better than all that Apollyon stood for. After some debate Apollyon "broke out into a grievous rage, saying, I am an enemy to this Prince; I hate his person, his laws and people; I am come out on purpose to withstand thee."

Christian replied, "Apollyon. Beware what you do; for I am in the king's highway, the way of holiness; therefore take heed to yourself."

Then Apollyon straddled quite over the whole breadth of the way, and said, "I am void of fear in this matter: prepare thyself to die; for I swear by my infernal den, that thou shalt go no further; here will I spill thy soul."

Those who sign up for engagement in this war, in the company of this Prince have purposed to engage in a war that's for heroes.

Yes, yes, I know how corny that sounds to those who have not yet seen the reality of the world through the lens of the cross of Christ. Ignoring the sneers and jeers we still know who the salt of the earth is. Of some of our heroic mothers and fathers Hebrews 11:38 says, "the world was not worthy of them." Now you can't get cornier than that! But then again, maybe Hollywood doesn't always know what a hero is.

*I'd hate the thoughts of the reader to degenerate into making this "a white and black thing". I have a sense of the pain and shame of the history of so many of us white people in relation to many black people but this gorgeous piece of George's history rises way beyond that. It implies his poverty but I'm white and Irish, born in the late 30's, one of thirteen children and I know about in-your-face poverty (as millions still do). But while that hovers around George's experience, the piece isn't about poverty or deprivation or past mistreatments for which people should repent on their knees. It's about joy!*

# *37*

## GEORGE DAWSON'S MULE AND WAGON

George Dawson died a few years back but not before he reached 103 years old and walked without a cane, he told us. A sweet-spirited black gentleman. He was a good boy that grew into a good man. I never met him but I know it would have been a privilege. When he was a little boy his friend Pete gave him a baseball. (Pete was later lynched by irate white people.) When George was a twenty-one year old man he went north to find a job and got one working at building levees. They told him to pick out the mule and wagon that he wanted. The mule's name was Joe. George's job was to go get dirt and rocks that would act as filler and come back to the levee and pour it all in the right place. He spoke of "his" mule and "his wagon". He explains. "I say 'my wagon,' because when I clucked at Joe to follow along behind Henry's wagon I was so excited about 'my wagon' and 'my mule' as if I was a kid and not a man of twenty-one years of age. I may have been grinning like a kid, but I felt like a man, all right. I admit it. With my own mule and wagon, I was mighty proud of myself. I had never really owned anything of my own, except for Peter's baseball. And I knew that wagon and mule were mine, at least as long as I was working there."

I'd hate the thoughts of the reader to degenerate into making this "a white and black thing". I have a sense of the pain and shame of the history of so many of us white people in relation to many black people but this gorgeous piece of George's history rises way beyond that. It implies his poverty but I'm white and Irish, born in the late 30's, one of thirteen children and I know about in-your-face poverty (as millions still do). But while that hovers around George's experience, the piece isn't about poverty or deprivation or past mistreatments for which people should repent on their knees. It's about joy! It's about the loveliness of self-respect. It's about the sweet pleasure of honourable success. His passing remark of comparison—sweeter because it is a passing remark—underscores the poignancy of the whole scene and the emotions of it. "I had never really owned anything of my own, except for Peter's baseball." Twenty-one years of age and had never owned anything but a baseball a friend gave him and now "my" mule and "my" wagon.

Haven't you—oh I hope you have—at some point in your life felt what George felt at that moment? The sheer can't-keep-from-grinning pleasure of having broken through a barrier, of rising higher than you had reason to think you might? I remember vividly when Roger Bannister broke the four-minute mile barrier. The thought of it pleases me but George's mule and wagon beats it all to pieces. Ah, sometimes life hands you a lovely piece of news and it makes more than your day—it brightens your life. This sweet man still thrilled at it more than eighty years later.

What can you remember?

# 38

## "DUZ YIR MAJESTY KNOW..."

Many years ago, the west coast of Ireland, a pompous marquis out for a walk so the villagers can have the privilege of seeing him. A boy, one sock up and the other down, cap at a rakish angle, well-worn shoes, short pants held up with suspenders passes the marquis by with barely a glance.

Offended by the absence of appreciation! A thunderous roar, "Boy!" Startled eyes look at the human volcano.

"Do you know who I am?"

A trembling response, "No sor. Indade I do noat!"

"Well, I'm the marquis!"

A respectful touch of the cap. "Pleased to meet yir honor, sor!"

Content now that the offence was dealt with the marquis resumed his self-satisfied way to the village center.

Fast recovering our young hero let him get a safe distance away before he shouted after him, "An' duz yir majesty know who I am? I'm Willie John Murphy from the house down by the boag! That's who I am!" And off he went with a swagger, his shoulders straighter and his thumbs hooked in his suspenders.

A healthy sense of one's personal worth is essential to a full life. You understand I'm not talking about an insistence in getting all our rights (who ever gets them all?) or an over-zealous awareness that we're as good as the next one. Willie John wanted the marquis know that he wasn't the only one due some respect.

There's something senseless as well as distasteful in snobbery or elitism. It equates wealth with character, education with wisdom or pedigree with quality. It suggests that the poor are pathetic, that those who aren't physical marvels are to be pitied or that those who don't score high on the mental acuity tests are hardly worth bothering with. What nonsense it is to be arrogant because you happened to be born into a prominent family. What bilge it is to think that only those who have climbed high mountains or trekked deep into some vast forest or gained celebrity status in the music or sports world have lived grand lives.

It's almost amusing (but not quite!) to see those of us with an inherited creed strut and crow because our understanding of truth is greater than that of our former friends who still remain in the realm of the "happy pagans". How blind are those of us who swagger because we buy our clothes in highbrow shops, attend upper-crust schools, have read more books, can lift more weight, can run faster, jump higher, look prettier or hold a job that is more influential than someone else's.

How can we not be pleased when we are blessed with such benefits? I know no crime in that and I don't believe we should work to make people feel guilty because they are so blessed—are these not gifts of God and honorable worked for?

It's the swagger, the arrogance, the scorn, the condescending air or the body language that speaks volumes about how we view those "beneath" us.

There lies the crime.

I don't say that character is *everything* because there is truth that transcends all our capacity to embody it. There is truth beyond and outside us that enables us to recognize grand character when we see it and if it did not exist we wouldn't know what good character is if we saw it. No, I don't say good character is everything but it beats all to pieces being able to run faster or climb higher or preach better than anyone else.

If we want someone to look after our children while we're away on some trip we won't ask them if they're expert at rock-climbing or whether they are amillennial or premillennial in their theology. First and foremost we would want to know if we could trust them with the care of our children. We might need to know if they had certain skills or a certain level of adequacy but if they were as competent as Florence Nightingale or as smart as Aristotle we'd still want to be sure we could trust our children to their care—are they of good character?

But even that truth does not go deep enough because there are many weary men and women who long for cleaner, braver and calmer lives; people whose battle with the darker side of their own souls have been too long with so little apparent success. A moral snob can drive such people into a permanent state of trembling or complete paralysis.

Our personal sense of worth must be grounded on bedrock or it will be eroded. The Hebrew—Christian scriptures will insist that the bedrock is God himself and the NT will announce that all hope of transformation now and a happy ending is grounded in *Jesus' integrity* (*dia pisteos tou Iesou Christou—Romans 3:22, Galatians 3:20, Philippians 3:9*)

And those who have not given their lives to God in the Lord Jesus need to know that God thinks them well worth pursuing to rescue. They need to know that he has come looking for them to both deliver them from sin and raise them to fullness of life in and through the Lord Jesus.

Willie John Murphy straightened the swollen marquis in his own way we can all insist before all who think we're worthless that God in and through Jesus doesn't think us so. Maybe the cross of the Lord Jesus trumps the fact that we don't have the right labels on our clothes!

*Loneliness, social isolation, the sense of being unwanted, the absence of tenderness, tender words, touches and kisses and glances—how could life not be tough in the absence of these? Those who have a profound need for such gifts but don't experience them wage an uphill battle and those who are in a happy and honorable and fulfilling romance should take that into account rather than assuming that their own religious devotion would be as easy to maintain or as real and deep if they were without a lovely companion.*

# *39*

## I FELT LIKE DANCING

Down the years I tried to persuade my Ethel that I'm not worth much and God knows I've behaved badly enough to have made my point with some others. She wasn't buying it—seems she heard that God thinks I'm worth dying for.

Still, what I'm about to say is risky and those who have known the worst side of me on occasions (should they by some remote chance ever read *anything* I write) will curl their lip at the next few remarks because they'll make me sound like Mr. Wonderful—fat chance of that being true!

If I hadn't already been in love with Ethel, listening to Rod Stewart's version of the old classic *Long Ago & Far Away* would have made me *want* to be in love. I who have never danced felt like dancing when I listened to it.

I've never forgotten the power of romance—I'm not built to be able to do that—but I haven't always remembered how warming and enriching and sustaining a lovely romance can be.

Many Christians tend to think—so I judge—that everyone has an equal chance to live life in the celebration mode. I know better; and so should they! Loneliness, social isolation, the sense of being unwanted, the absence of tenderness, tender words, touches and kisses and glances—how could life not be tough in the absence of these? Those who have a profound need for such gifts but don't experience them wage an uphill battle and those who are in a happy and honorable and fulfilling romance should take that into account rather than assuming that their own religious devotion would be as easy to maintain or as real and deep if they were without a lovely companion. (It makes no sense for us to rejoice in a gift God has given us and at the same time begrudge it to the entire human family. Instead of berating people for enjoying romance maybe we should remind them that it's God's gift to them.)

I accept the fact that we as a society are excessively interested in sex and all the "liberties" that go with it but that truth shouldn't lead us to idiotic conclusions. We shouldn't deny the richness of the gift God has offered to us as humans in offering us romance. And I'm aware that there are those who are in relationships that are crushing them—a tragic circumstance; but none of that is what I wish to deal with here. I just feel the need to express my pleasure at the sound of music and the warmth of romance.

To dismiss the sheer pleasure in a love relationship between two people is to do more than God would do. He uses the metaphors of marriage and romance, of human lovers and happy brides and bridegrooms to express his own joy and when he came to us in and as Jesus he was no stranger to the happy mystery of a wedding.

As it is, I have a difficult enough time trying to please God and be like him; but if I were without the joys of a loving relationship—I'm talking about **me**—I don't think I could make it.

I think my Ethel used to dance when she was a girl and before she died I often wished she could get out of her wheelchair and show me how. Oh well. A couple of times I put Rod Stewart on and mimed the words to her. It set her little heart all aflutter, don't you know.

# *40*

## Abel Magwitch

How could a person make his way through life with any success with the name Magwitch? Isn't that a burden all by itself? The first time I met Abel Magwitch he was hiding and wandering in a marshy area down by the sea near a lonely graveyard. He was hiding from the police and he was on the lookout for a fellow-prisoner—he was an escaped convict, you see. That's when he came across a boy called Phillip Pirrip. Frightened the life out of him he did. The child could never seem to get his tongue around his name and he said it came out more like "Pip" so maybe it wasn't surprising that the name "Pip" stuck.

Magwitch, a violent man with a violent and criminal background, threatened the child with all sorts of dire consequences if he didn't come back to him with food and a file so that he could file off his chains. He made the terrified boy swear an awful oath and assured him that his liver would be roasted and eaten if he didn't keep to the oath. The child was scared witless so he said nothing to his sister with whom he lived (along with her husband, blacksmith

Joe Gargery, Pip's parents being dead). He took some food and a file from Joe's forge and sneaked off to the evil Abel Magwitch who devoured the food and spoke roughly to the boy. Did he tell anyone? Was he followed? Was he going to tell? More threats of dire consequences. Later there were police at the house. They were looking for two escaped convicts and Pip was terrified but kept his mouth shut though worse was to follow. There was the stolen food, another crime added to previous crimes, only now it was Pip who was the thief so he feared not only the convict but the police since he had given help to a criminal. Shouts and sounds said that they had caught the ruffians and as the crowd gathered the hard-bitten Magwitch eyed the frightened boy, knew he hadn't betrayed him and claimed that *he* had stolen the food and the file. They took him away. Far away; a world away—to Australia.

Life went on, the fear and excitement was only a memory and in the passing months and years Pip fell in love with the beautiful Estella whom he met at the old, gloomy, frozen-in-the-past house of Miss Haversham. Miss Haversham, Pip came to believe, was nurturing him so that one day he would be Estella's husband and when a lawyer from London, an acquaintance of Miss H, informed Pip that he was to receive a regular income and be raised as a gentleman he knew where it was coming from.

Pip's love for Estella wasn't returned but still (as Pip thought) Miss H continued to provide an abundant supply of money so that Pip could live in ease while he studied and became cultured. The young man later discovered that Miss Havisham was only using him as a whipping boy, spitefully punishing him for what a man had done to her years ago when he both swindled and then jilted her. Where, then, was all the money coming from?

One stormy night a scary figure came knocking at Pip's door and in walked this fierce stranger who turned out to be the desperate criminal the boy had met on the wild marshland. The young man was scared witless but he didn't need to be afraid because Magwitch meant him no harm—no harm at all. In a few moments, with pointed questions, the ex-convict revealed to Pip that it was he who all along had made life easy and had been paying for Pip's growth as a man of culture and learning. The stunned Pip listened in fright and astonishment as Magwitch exulted in Pip's progress and his part in it.

"Yes, Pip, dear boy, I've made a gentleman on you! It's me wot has done it! I swore that time, sure as ever I earned a guinea that guinea should go to you. I swore arterwards, sure as ever I spec'lated and got rich, you should get rich. I lived rough, that you should live smooth; I worked hard that you should be above work. What odds, dear boy? Do I tell it fur you to feel a obligation? Not a bit. I tell it, fur you to know as that there hunted dunghill dog wot you kept life in, got his head so high that he could make a gentleman—and Pip, you're him…When I was a hired-out shepherd in a solitary hut, not seeing no faces but the faces of the sheep till I half forgot wot men's and women's faces wos like, I see yourn. I drops my knife many a time in that hut when I was a eating my dinner or my supper, and I says, 'Here's the boy again, a looking at me whiles I eats and drinks!' I see you there many times as plain as ever I see you on the misty marshes. 'Lord strike me dead!' I says each time—and I goes out in the open air to say it under the open heavens—'but wot, if I gets liberty and money, I'll make that boy a gentleman!' And I done it."

Don't you love it when you see such a change? Aren't you happy for the boy and for numerous reasons even happier for the man whose life turned around and became one of honest toil out of a cheerful heart? Isn't it marvelous to hear of a single purpose, a single glorious purpose that took over and drove someone along the road of honor and selflessness?

A life that lacks an overarching purpose, a primary motivation that is served, in one way or another, by all other motives and purposes—a life like that is lacking a fundamental element. An old ex-convict called Magwitch makes such a life look shallow.

If a surgeon with a scalpel had dug down into Paul's chest until he reached the heart of his heart he would have found written on it:

## For Jesus Christ!

I wonder what…

*The Exodus shoves the curtain aside and generations live in the strength of that vision. The Incarnation catches us by the breath and the Cross drives us to joyful amazement. Paul, on whom the shadow of the cross fell, was driven, careering off across half a world to proclaim triumph and hope in the name of the God who was hung on a public gallows*

# 41

## CRIPPLED TRUTHS WILL WALK

Seamus Heaney adapted a play of Sophocles called "Philoctetes". The central character is Philoctetes, a Greek hero who possessed a charmed bow and arrows given to him by Hercules. On the island of Lemnos a serpent bit him and his foot began to rot. The intolerable pain made him scream all the time and the stench from the foot became unbearable to those around him so they deserted him. He endured ten years of loneliness, pain and the anguish of betrayal. Days became weeks, weeks became months and months became years and hope of rescue faded as his bitterness grew. But an oracle told the Greeks they couldn't take Troy without the bow of Philoctetes so they went back to ask him if he would go with them. His years of disappointed hope were over and when he emptied himself of the bitterness that had built up inside him the cripple marched off with them to glory.

Heaney puts these words in the mouths of the chorus at the end of the play: "History forbids us to hope this side of the grave. But once in a lifetime, the longed-for tide of justice can arise and hope and history rhyme." With Northern Ireland as its setting, with its long history of feuds and killings, dashed hopes, treachery and unfulfilled promises, Heaney's call was well contextualized and however limited the changes in Northern Ireland help us to believe other chronically sick situations can change in a country, a church or a life.

So while there's a God like the one exhibited in Jesus Christ don't cease to hope because one day hope and history will rhyme and crippled truths will walk!

Much of history is humdrum. Some of it is random (But God is the Lord of randomness)! Much of it forbids us to hope this side of the grave. Some biblical history shares these features. Not every event recorded in the Bible is filled with theological significance but here and there, an event or a cluster of events seizes our attention and God has reached from behind the curtain of his hiddenness and in these events we catch a glimpse of him. And once we've seen him we can't "unsee" him.

The Exodus shoves the curtain aside and generations live in the strength of that vision. The Incarnation catches us by the breath and the Cross drives us to joyful amazement. Paul, on whom the shadow of the cross fell, was driven, careering off across half a world to proclaim triumph and hope in the name of the God who was hung on a public gallows. And when friendly hands would try to slow Paul down, telling him to take it easy, he would shrug them off and say: "I can't be different, the love of Christ compels me and the world needs hope." (2 Corinthians 5:14)

And it doesn't matter that we moderns hang Christ again and again, thinking we've got rid of him, he's been there and done that! Christ can't be harmed by crucifixion. In fact there's every reason to believe that he is never as powerful as he is when he's weak so to crucify him over again is in some ways to turn him loose on society. Even to see him crucified (when we trouble the church, which is his body) is to put ourselves in danger of being drawn to him because he said when he was "lifted up from the earth" he would draw all men unto him. That cross...that strange cross.

# 42

## A VOICE IN FAR-FLUNG GALAXIES

1 Corinthians 1:5-6 has this: "For in him you have been enriched in every way—in all your speech and in all your knowledge—because our testimony about Christ was confirmed in you."

They had been enriched in "every way". Paul then illustrates what he means by isolating speech and knowledge and, of course, what is true of the Corinthians is true of all who are in Jesus Christ.

It's fashionably wise and spiritual to dismiss speech and knowledge as mere surface issues. Christ didn't take such an approach and neither did Paul. Christ said his words were spirit and truth and he said that knowing the one true God and his Son, Jesus Christ, was eternal life. Paul knew the dangers of knowledge and the vanity of words but the cure for such abuse and vanity is not ignorance and speechlessness. It isn't wise to be wiser or more spiritual than God. In the passage above he says Christ enriches our speech.

We're enriched in Christ in our speech. When his influence in us has its way cheap and sleazy talk leaves the building. Our stories are cleaner, truer and funnier (in part because they're cleaner); they carry people's minds down better avenues and generate pleasure and joy without being tasteless and crude. Our life stories are enriched because our master Story is far and away the best, the most enthralling, the most adventurous, the most mystifying and the most hopeful of all master stories. The Story is cosmic as well as personal; it affects how we see the darkest corridors of space and the way we look at little children; it gives us a sense of mission and destiny as it cultivates strength and calls us to moral heroism.

In Jesus Christ we're enriched because we have something to talk about that dwarfs all the social programs (even good social programs) while it careers us headlong into rich social engagement and change, as agents of change for Jesus' sake. In Jesus Christ we have something to say to a chattering Western world that can make its voice heard in far-flung galaxies but has nothing worth saying!

# 43

## PARADISE CAN BE HERE TOO

I confess to being melancholic and while the description of the Irish poet W.B Yeats may be too strong to describe me I still think it moves somewhat in the right direction. It was said of him: "Being Irish, he had an abiding sense of tragedy, which sustained him through temporary periods of joy."

If you think this might be another piece of emotional striptease I'd quit reading it right now and move to something more to your liking for I'm inclined to think that that's what it is—but then again, maybe…

I'm not sure!

I've felt the need recently to write more about my Ethel in particular and, more generally, about life and relationships, romance and friendship, creation blessings as the gifts of God that are not to be despised or even simply "accepted". Some of us aren't able, due to limiting factors past and present, to be pleased with life much less "dance like a Dervish." I can understand that but I would insist that our inability to exult in human existence should have some genuine causes rather than the false notion that life here on earth isn't truly "living" and that that's how God meant it to be—as if we're merely marking time until we get to heaven and then we'll *really* live. *That isn't the Bible's message at all!*

I fully believe that there is no **fullness** of life without life in God and I'm acutely aware that there are those who worship pleasure and so are "dead while they live." All that I take for granted. But to rejoice fully in the present life as a gift of God that is tied up in his purposes for us is what the biblical witness calls us to do. When Christians feel reluctant to let themselves go and enjoy the earthy nature of God's gift it isn't because *God* wants them to be reluctant—they get that from somewhere else.

The "heaven" of popular tradition (which pretty much takes the images in Revelation as a literal description of our future existence) doesn't compete with the joy of our present life's honorable and loving relationships. God is (so to speak) astonished at those who say they love him and don't love their earthly companions in Jesus (see 1 John 4:20—why do you think he would say such a thing?).

To commit to someone and have them commit to you, to be companions to each other in joy and pain, in sore years and years of smiles and happiness—all that is wondrous. To watch and learn from each other, to be enriched by one another, to be rescued, forgiven, called to courage and manliness, to righteousness and to be received with warm affection—this is "life". To be able to exchange knowing smiles, to laugh together until your stomach hurts, to love passionately and to miss the other when they're gone so that you don't feel "complete"—this is "living".

No wonder the songwriter in the old song, *The Sunshine of Your Smile* makes the lover speak of his beloved's dear face and say, "Were you not mine/How dark the night would be/I know no light above that can replace/Love's radiant sunshine in your own dear face." He goes on to say, "Give me your smile/The love light in your eyes/Life cannot not hold a fairer paradise." The thought of heaven does nothing for this lover in comparison with the heaven he finds with his beloved and it's easy in our piety to find fault with that but sometimes we Christians try too hard! No one will deny that to be with Christ is better but humans are humans, and God himself acknowledges that (see again 1 John 4:20).

So let's keep our hearts tuned centrally to God so that our love of our loved ones will not get between him and us. Let's accept the fact that some things are passing without despising the present reality or our bodies which God will raise to immortality in Jesus Christ. Let's not be ashamed of our deep sense of present loss if our loved ones leave us in death, even though we know that partings in Jesus are never the final word (see 1 Thessalonians 4:13).

I think that I'm presently trying to come to terms with the depth of my emotion toward my Ethel—an emotional depth I've never felt toward God. I continue to sometimes literally tremble when I remember that she died. I understand, don't you know, that she and I are friends forever and that death can't harm two people like us who have found and been found by God in Jesus Christ. That truth is never destroyed by my (near panic) it's just that the fear-filled emotions push the everlasting truths aside for a time when I would ask myself how I'd hold together if she should die. [I think then of David Gates' song: *Lost Without Your Love* which moves in a slightly different direction but still expresses a devastating sense of loss at love lost.]

If God reads this piece I'm not *certain* what he'll think of it but I'm committing it to him anyway in the hope that he's not at all unhappy that I feel what I feel and that he thinks it does him no disservice.

*What pleasure does God get out of us? He loves it when we say no to the God-denying look of the world. It gives him pleasure to see us struggle against great odds, continually lose specific battles and still get back up and into the war.*

# 44

## It matters to God!

It makes sense for someone to say it doesn't matter to God whether we like him or not. But that would only be one more "sensible" thing that's wrong because it does matter to God whether we like him or not. That's an astonishing truth about God which, when we think about it in the light of creation and redemption in Christ, becomes obvious. How could he in love create us and not care what we think about him? It's true enough that he can be angry and chastise us but that only proves that it matters to him what we think about him! Revelation 3:19 says he chastises us because he loves us!

One of the awful lies Job's friend Eliphaz told was this: "It doesn't matter to God how you behave or think. It doesn't affect him one way or another." (See Job 22:2-3.) As the NIV renders it Eliphaz says, "Can a man be of benefit to God? Can even a wise man benefit him? What pleasure would it give the Almighty if you were righteous? What would he gain if your ways were blameless?" Eliphaz means well. He wants to exalt God far above all the puniness of humanity but in the process he bears false witness against God because the whole book of Job is built on the fact that God is proud of Job (see 1:8 and 2:3 and 42:7-8).

What pleasure does God get out of us? He loves it when we say no to the God-denying look of the world. It gives him pleasure to see us struggle against great odds, continually lose specific battles and still get back up and into the war. And we do battle against great odds. We've been shaped in wickedness, we've come to love ease and take great pleasure in feathering our present and post-mortem nests. We've been dominated by patterns of behavior for many years and there's enough evil in the world to continue to feed those patterns that makes them hard to break.

Poverty and war, social evils and paramilitaries, entrenched corruption in government, ill-health and depression come at us, wave after wave. Now and then we sense the awful power of the Sin that has the world by the throat and it's then we see the cross for what it is. All these awful evils that we can see and sense remind us that there is something deeper, more awful than these visible horrors; they're the tip of the iceberg. So when you stand up, when you shut your mouth to vile speech, when you open your hand in generosity, when you open your heart in forgiveness, when you dismiss the temptation to isolate yourself from the church and the needy world, it matters to God. It pleases him! More than that, it advances his cosmic purposes. You are fighting God's battle for him against all the forces of gloom and cynicism in the world. One day you will see the glory of what you have done!

**Believe it: it matters to God!**

# 45

## WHAT WE HAVE TO OFFER

Believers have profound reasons to rejoice because what they have is more than "religion"—it's *life!*

Sin is always a madman's choice. Flinging away from Jesus is always the final madness. There came a point in Judas's life when he looked at the thirty pieces of silver in his hand and hating himself for his stupidity and treachery he hurled them to the pavement and went out into the night and ended his life. It doesn't end so dramatically for all of us—some of us go silently to the grave or go whimpering. But however we go down, it doesn't matter what it was that we got in return for Christ, no, not even if it was the entire world for a million years. The time will come when we'll look at or around or in whatever we got and we'll see it, dry as dust, lifeless, without soul or joy, not a scrap to be proud of and we'll hear ourselves screaming in disbelief, "This? It was for this that I gave up God?"

We take pleasure in things according to how we've been shaped by experience and how we're made up; we find satisfaction in them depending on how grown or immature we are. An infant can't exult in Shakespeare, a miser can't rejoice in the absolute delight on the face of a needy person who has just been given a generous gift. And someone enslaved in bitterness can't know the profound pleasure that comes when he or she gives the gift of full and free forgiveness. Unless *we* are changed and grow we can't know the joy and pleasure in the things we have or experience or *could* engage in. If we don't change they forever remain the same and because that's so, by and by they become a bore and a burden. If we don't change we forever shut doors that could lead us to a mesmerizing world of inexpressible joy. Even hardened criminals find a deep satisfaction in doing what is "right" according to their standards. I'm sure that however far we've strayed from God we've all experienced a time when we "did the right thing". And every so often we bring that event out to look at it again and take pleasure in knowing that at least once in our lives the man or woman in us stood up and wouldn't bend!

Why should it surprise us that tens of millions shrug at the name Jesus and party on? At best, multiplied millions of us find him a bore, a killer of life. The church historian Theodoret tells us that the emperor Julian, as he died, groaned out that the Galilean carpenter had conquered. The poet Swinburne adds to it in *Hymn to Proserpine* when he says, "You have conquered pale Galilean, the whole world grows grey at your breath."

We're bored with Christ, bored with the message about him and bored with the people that represent him (even the ones worthy of him). There's too much life to get on with without him. There's too much to eat, to drink, to engage in, laugh about and experience to even bid him the time of day. If he offered *life* maybe we'd stop and talk with him a while but as it is, who wants a ceaseless cowing and groveling even to a God? Especially if he is a God of gloom and clearly, so we're told and so you would think if you listen to some believers—clearly Jesus was melancholy at best.

What a piece of nonsense! When bringing *life* to the needy and his critics jumped on him for it (Luke 15) Jesus told them he *loved* his work. He told them he felt like a shepherd that had found a precious sheep he had lost and wanted everyone to experience his joy. He told them he felt the way a sensitive woman feels when she finds a lost coin that has great value for her and he felt as a broken-hearted father feels when a beloved son comes back to life. On one occasion we're told that his disciples told him of the great good they had done for the land and it filled Jesus to the brim with joy! ("Yes, but that's what I mean. Now we're back to mere religion." Hmmm, try telling that to singer Bob Geldof—no friend of religion—who found deep joy in helping the terribly needy.)

It isn't necessary, you understand, for Christians to pretend that they enjoy all the things everyone else enjoys in order to make Christ attractive. *[Isn't it a pathetic sight when we see believers trying too hard to prove that they're "ordinary Joes"?]* Down below all the tasty things, there is life that lacks no joy and it's found in one whose vision embraced all the harmless, pleasure-bringing joys of life and thought they were God's gifts. But he's the one that told the story about a couple of men who knew greater treasure when they saw it: a farm laborer and a pearl merchant. Filled with the excitement of the find they had to have it though it meant dispensing with other lesser things. When these two men began selling all they had some might have thought they were mad but they knew that now that their eyes were opened they *would* be mad if they *didn't* sell all. Joy drove them to it!

Christians are not competing with the non-believing world at the level of entertainment. We're bearing witness to *fullness* of life. Cheating nobody while we long to enrich all by the one reality that makes every good pleasure even more pleasant—Jesus Christ!

#####

Jim McGuiggan
holywoodjk@aol.com
www.jimmcguiggan.com/
Weaver Publications
Beth Weaver
330 317-3223

www.ingramcontent.com/pod-product-compliance
Lightning Source LLC
Chambersburg PA
CBHW060325050426
42449CB00011B/2658